THE WAY YOU DO
ANYTHING
IS
THE WAY YOU DO
EVERYTHING

THE WAY YOU DO ANYTHING IS THE WAY YOU DO EVERYTHING

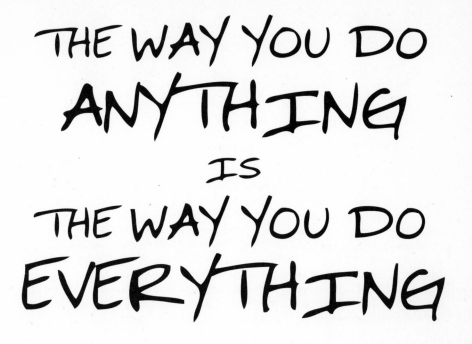

THE **WHY** OF
WHY YOUR BUSINESS
ISN'T MAKING MORE MONEY

SUZANNE EVANS

WILEY

Cover design: Wiley

Published by John Wiley & Sons, Inc., Hoboken, New Jersey.
Published simultaneously in Canada.

For general information about our other products and services, please contact our Customer Care Department within the United States at (800) 762-2974, outside the United States at (317) 572-3993 or fax (317) 572-4002.

Wiley publishes in a variety of print and electronic formats and by print-on-demand. Some material included with standard print versions of this book may not be included in e-books or in print-on-demand. If this book refers to media such as a CD or DVD that is not included in the version you purchased, you may download this material at http://booksupport.wiley.com. For more information about Wiley products, visit www.wiley.com.

ISBN 978-1-118-71426-3 (cloth); ISBN 978-1-118-71429-4 (ebk);
ISBN 978-1-118-71432-4 (ebk)

Printed in the United States of America.

10 9 8 7 6 5 4 3 2 1

*For Dad and his daily enthusiasm; and
for Mom, who never gives up.*

Contents

CONTENTS

Foreword

Suzanne Evans is a force of nature. She's smart. She's insightful. She's tough. She's hilarious. She is willing to do whatever it takes to get the results she wants. She demands the best from herself and from others. With Suzanne, there is no excuse big enough to knock her off course. And she has the proverbial heart of gold.

Those are all pretty nice things to say considering that I refused to talk to her for nearly a year. Yep, it's true. Suzanne contacted me, wanting me to coach her on helping her build her brand. At first I ignored her. Then I put her off, both politely and sometimes not so politely. I even gave her a big flat out *No!*, but Suzanne is a very persistent person. She just wouldn't let up. She ignored my *no* and kept after me, and she made such a compelling argument that she eventually wore me down, and I finally agreed to meet with her. I am so glad I did.

She flew to Scottsdale, Arizona, and met with me for a full day at my house. We sat at my dining room table and got to know each other. I found her to be a total delight. She was funny, charismatic, and focused. She was completely open and willing to learn. Like all great teachers, she is an amazing student. That is a great lesson for everyone right there! But what I learned that mattered most to me during that initial time with Suzanne was that she lives her life and runs her business grounded in the principles of honesty, fairness, and integrity. Those elements are missing in society and business for sure, but they seem to especially be missing in the business she and I are both in. As you can tell, Suzanne won me over completely. I quickly moved from mentor to friend to fan.

In this book, Suzanne has a lot to teach you. You will hear her amazing story of how she went from a secretarial job that was neither personally or professionally fulfilling to being on the Inc. 500 list of fastest growing companies in less than four years. She grabbed life by the throat and created opportunities so she could live the life she had always dreamed of. Have you ever wished you could do that? If that alone doesn't get your attention and make you want to learn from her, then nothing will.

You are about to learn the ideas and principles she uses in her life, and how she uses those principles to build her business and create a dedicated following of fans and customers. What you are going to love about this book is that you are going to read it and say to yourself, "I can do that!" And you are right, you can. The question is never, "Can you?" but is always, "Will you?" If you are ready to take action and change your life and your business, then you have certainly come to the right book and the right person. I am excited for you to learn from my great friend, the amazing Suzanne Evans!

—Larry Winget,
The Pitbull of Personal Responsibility®,
television personality, and five-time *New York Times/Wall Street Journal* bestselling author of such books as *Grow A Pair* and *Shut Up, Stop Whining and Get A Life*

Acknowledgments

When you finish writing a book, you feel like you want to thank everyone. It certainly takes a village. So I will go the wuss route to start and thank all the friends, family, and colleagues that have always believed in me and supported me. That should cover everyone.

And now I will get specific.

To Matt and all of the wonderful folks at Wiley that were patient with a very "green" author. I appreciate your guidance, support, and direction.

To Fran and Barry Weissler for taking a chance on me 14 years ago in a job I was not ready for, probably did not deserve, and wasn't sure how to perform. Then, for teaching me how to make money, run a business, and always turn things around, and land on your feet. I learned more in that office listening to meetings and phone calls and negotiations than anyone could learn at Harvard. Thank you.

To my Hell Yeah Team at Suzanne Evans Coaching. Every day they make me look good and be better than I am. You are hardworking, dedicated, and caring. You are not just a team, but family.

To the mentors that have really mattered in my life.... David Neagle for inspiring the beliefs in this book, Adam Urbanski for opening my eyes to marketing, and Larry Winget for getting me to write, getting it published, and making it finally happen.

To my clients. How did I get lucky enough to learn more than I teach? It's an honor to be allowed into people's businesses and lives. I never take it for granted and it brings me joy every day.

To my sister, Amanda. Most of the time when I write I am hoping to be as smart as her. When I give back I am hoping to be as generous as her. When I dress I am hoping to be as cute as her. When I work I am hoping to be as tenacious as her. She's an inspiration and the love of my life.

To my Mom and Dad, Sue and Johnnie Evans, for all the reasons most people thank their parents. I got amazing support, good advice, and endless love. But I got something inspiring time and time again (even when I did not deserve it). Pride. The pride they have had in me and all I have done is still surprising at times. It has made me feel so special, and in the end that's what we all want—to have someone be proud of us.

And, finally, to the person who makes all of this worth it. My partner, Melonie, has made all the late nights, failed ideas, celebrations, tragedies, and triumphs mean something. Simply because she was there. Every time and without fail. It would be impossible to match her support. I hope that everyone gets one person in their life to believe in them the way she has believed in me. I got exceptionally lucky because that kind of belief makes it easier to keep going.

THE WAY YOU DO
ANYTHING
IS
THE WAY YOU DO
EVERYTHING

Introduction

When my mom suffered a significant stroke a few years ago, I hastily made the three-hour trip to be with her.

The employees at the local hospital were kind and helpful, but also wildly disorganized and reactionary. My mother lay uncomfortably, without decent sheets or a warm enough blanket, for a day and a half while the hospital searched for a bed. After 36 hours without a wink of sleep, she finally got one in the intensive-care unit (ICU).

Once she was settled in, it felt as if a hundred questions a minute were flying at me. This wasn't easy; I was getting advice and recommendations from six different doctors, sandwiched between multiple procedures. It was an incredibly trying time.

I kept trying to pull all the pieces together in the hopes of making the right decisions for Mom. I was focused on saving her life and getting her well.

Something felt off, though. I thought that if I headed home to get a couple hours of sleep, I might figure out what it was. As I laid my head on the pillow, I thought to myself: *The way you do anything is the way you do everything.*

That's when it hit me: If the people at this hospital aren't competent enough to get my mother a blanket, I certainly didn't want them providing critical care to her. The way they achieved (or, in this case,

1

failed to achieve) this one simple task was the way they'd handle all others, and that didn't instill a great deal of confidence in me.

I jumped out of bed and immediately began making phone calls. I knew I needed to transfer my mother to another hospital, Duke Medical Center. In about eight hours, we were in an ambulance en route to Durham, North Carolina. When we arrived, a patient family director greeted us and guided us to the family area, where he proceeded to inform us of the amenities for families of patients in the ICU. After only 10 minutes, I already felt better.

The staff's efficiency and calm demeanor were amazing. After my mom was admitted, when I was allowed to see her, I bent down, kissed her, and asked her if she needed anything. She replied, "I am still cold."

I saw a slender, quick-moving gentlemen float around me to ask, "Did she say she was cold?" It was Nick, her private nurse for the evening. Before I even knew what had happened, he turned on his heel, went around the corner and returned with a blanket. And he hadn't just grabbed it from a closet in the hall. This blanket had just come from a *warming bin*.

He opened it up, swaddled her, and I saw my mother smile for the first time in three days. Not only did they get her a blanket, but it was also warm. It seemed like a small detail, but at that moment, it made all the difference in the world. I knew she was already getting better.

The way you do anything is the way you do everything.

● ● ●

What separates excellence from average is not talent or opportunity. It is *approach*. There are business owners, and then there is Richard Branson. There are basketball players, and then there is Michael Jordan. There are hospitals, and then there is Duke Medical Center.

The staff at Duke could have brought my mom a normal blanket, but that would have been average. Approach and attention to every detail with equal and consistent enthusiasm and commitment is what creates wild success, in both organizations and individuals.

Those who struggle in business frequently shift the blame to others for their shortcomings. We blame customers for not paying enough or buying enough. We blame marketing and sales for not making magic when we expect them to. We blame the economy for, well, *everything*. But the truth is you have everything you will ever need to create more money for your organization. It rests in the details of how you are living your life, treating your staff, talking to your kids, and showing up.

The way you do anything is the way you do everything.

My own entrepreneurial path as a business and marketing coach has given me a vast amount of opportunity to reflect on how to be successful—and how, for many years, I personally avoided success at all costs.

Back in 2005, I was working as an assistant for a Broadway production company. Anyone in the industry knows that *assistant* is just a fancy name for secretary. I was earning about $45,000 a year and living in New York City, where the cost of living is double that of most other places.

I was bored, broke, confused, and almost $100,000 in debt. I was a classic example of someone who made bad decisions, was afraid, and took nothing in my life seriously enough to make real change. I wish I remembered the precise moment I recognized this truth. After months of knowing something had to change, but having no idea how to change it, I heard this advice: In order for anything to change, you have to change *yourself*.

This immediately pissed me off because it forced me to face the truth. My problems weren't due to bad luck, bad breaks, or chance. It was *me*.

It was every decision I had made to that point in my life, every choice that had gotten me further from where I wanted to be. One day while building a vision board at work (I know it's cliché to build a vision board and wrong to build one at work, but I was doing it anyway), I came across the quote: *The way you do anything is the way you do everything.* In that moment, it all became clear: If I change the way I do things, those *things* will inevitably change.

Over the next six months, I got honest about my finances and tracked my spending habits. I got realistic and about my health, and lost some weight. I got clear on the business I wanted to build. I wasn't fully sure about every detail, but I knew I could help people. I knew I had an ability to solve problems; and people had a lot of problems. Even without all the details—I knew I could do life coaching.

And I begin to realize, *wow*, this *actually works.*

As I shifted my perspective, I saw more opportunities than obstacles. As my business grew, I matured, and I actually forgot about that quote for a while. A few years later, I realized I needed to hire a coach for myself. When I went to see him speak during a seminar of about 300 people, that life-changing advice came back to me. My new coach said, "The way you do anything is the way you do everything."

It was the line of thinking that had gotten me out of misery so many years before, and then I thought it just might get me to the next level. I made a commitment to live by that quote and take 100% responsibility for everything:

- How I treated myself.
- How I treated others.
- How I work.
- How I play.
- How I show up for an appointment.
- Even how I *feel.*

And that was the year my business grew to seven figures.

People ask me all the time how I made the Inc. 500 list, or how I went from a secretary to the owner of a multi-million dollar business in just 5 years. While I know these people want a hot marketing strategy or a secret plan, I don't have that because I didn't use anything like that. I just paid attention to everything I did and got caught up in the details of my life.

Every. Single. Detail.

I stopped focusing on my skills and talents, and started focusing on my commitment and my approach. I made one dollar at a time, and focused on one intention at a time, one idea at a time, and one get-back-up-and-go at a time.

I've heard the same story countless times from different people: You are bright, capable, ready, and yet you struggle with your business. People armed with little marketing knowledge and lots of passion launch businesses every day. And one fails every hour. Business acumen doesn't matter as much as *who you are* and how you play the game. Yes, I like to think of business as a game, because any other way of looking at it is just too daunting.

This book is for the people who have launched businesses without knowing what the hell they were doing or what to do next. It is for every entrepreneur who has the passion and has put in the work but can't seem to find the profits.

As Chief Pastor Reverend T. D. Jakes says, "Don't fuss at your children. They are a reflection of you." The same is true of your business; it is a reflection of you. Your profits mirror your choices. Your success mirrors your commitment. Your cash flow is a reflection of the consistency in everything in your life. Therefore, your business can change only if you change, and will only grow if you grow. And we grow by making smart choices.

I somehow muddled through, making my way from bored and broke to running a thriving business that I am incredibly passionate about—and I know you can, too. You don't *have* to muddle through. This book is a fast track to fixing *you*. Notice that I did not say fixing *your business*. This book can't possibly tackle all the potential challenges businesses face—but we can work on *you* and what you struggle with. And I can promise that in the process, your business will get better, bigger, and a hell of a lot more fun.

This book is *not* for people who believe that the economy, customers, or anyone else is to blame for their business's failures. It's also not for anyone who isn't willing to learn a thing or two. The formula for failure is to show up thinking you know everything and hoping you get something. This formula may be how you have been approaching your customers up until this point. This is a great opportunity to test *the way you do anything*.

Do you often wonder any of the following about your customers:

- Why are they so cheap?
- What can I get from them?
- Why are they so needy?
- Why do I have to walk them through *everything*?

Ever thought even just one of these? Probably, and that's part of the problem! Let this be your big *a-ha!* moment.

You should approach your customers the same way you should approach your life, which is the same way you will approach this book.

This book will *absolutely* help individuals who, like me, were *messed up*. The teachings and lessons within helped me, and it can help you, too, but only if you're prepared to believe that no one else messed you up. You need to come willing to recognize what you're doing wrong, own your mistakes, fix them, and start doing things right.

In my view, things are a lot simpler than you realize. That's the good news. The other news (we won't even call it *bad*) is that it is much harder work than you imagined it would be.

Even when your business reaches an amazing pace, you have to *keep* improving your dance moves or your business will quickly two-step out of your life.

As entrepreneurs, we have an amazing opportunity to shape the world, but we can only do it through expanding our thought process. Every success I have had (and every success you will have) is a reflection of our ability to expand our knowledge, to change our approach, and to adapt. It is not a reflection of your MBA, your invention, or even your past success, but of what you bring to the table. Your business is you.

Shall we get you on track?

CHAPTER 1

The Way You Do Anything...

But I have no mind for business and considered staying awake to be enough of an accomplishment.

—David Sedaris, *Me Talk Pretty One Day*

My dear friend and client Pat Mussieux followed me around the world for two years. She traveled anywhere I spoke just to ask me the same question over and over again. After two years, I finally told her, "I will only continue with you as a client if you stop asking me this question." She agreed.

Pat's question was: "So many of us want to build a successful business. How did you do it?" The answer I gave her never varied: It was about being extraordinary in everything I did.

When I think about being extraordinary—where that ability comes from and how you harness it—I think about being four years old. I was a little four-year-old, very small for my age. (Looking at the jacket cover, I know it's hard to imagine me ever being little, but back then, I was.) I also had extremely small feet. All year, I had been taking ballet lessons at Miss Anne Clark's School of Dance. I took those dance lessons very seriously. Then in spring, when weather started changing, excitement started growing. I traded my sweater for a long-sleeved T-shirt, and everything started to feel different because summer was on its way! It was time for Mother's Day, and preschool graduation, and the big dance recital. Even if you or your children haven't ever had recitals, you can probably imagine the feeling as the day draws closer.

I was pretty excited about my first performance; we had been rehearsing for months for this moment. My feet were so small that I couldn't wear the ballet slippers that all the other kids were wearing. I had to wear little white gymnast slippers because they couldn't find ballet shoes to fit me, but I didn't mind because the rest of my costume was so spectacular. I got to wear a little white tutu, and the best part about it was that it had a little shimmer to it. It also had a vest that laced up with red, yellow, and green satin ribbons, and a matching headpiece with the same color ribbons hanging down. In my mind, that was long hair, and I was Diana Ross. And as if a tremendous costume like this wasn't enough, I also got to have my hair and makeup done.

Soon, it was showtime. I was pretty nervous; there were only five of us in the class so we would all be in the front row, sharing the spotlight. We were also the first group to perform at the big recital.

Looking back, I realize the reason they put my group on first was because we were the little babies, and they didn't want us to have to wait through a two-hour recital before it was our turn to dance. You get the kids on, you get them off, and you get them home and in bed.

We were sitting backstage, nervous and playing and just being kids. All the parents were sitting backstage as well, giving much-needed encouragement: "Do your best. Do your best. You know this. You can do this." Meanwhile, they were thinking to themselves: "Don't embarrass me. Don't humiliate me. I've paid $78 a month for you to take these classes. Don't mess this up."

But you don't say *that* to a four-year-old.

When we were ready, all the parents went out and lined up with their cameras. They were probably even more eager and anxious than we were—on the edge of their seats to see their daughters' first dance recital.

The wranglers were backstage keeping us quiet and together in a group until the perfect moment when they pushed us onto the stage. And suddenly, there we were.

Our routine started in second position. Arms in circular position, and feet as wide as a four year old can make them. I felt ready. I told my four-year-old self, "I can do this. I got this. I got this. It's alright. Keep breathing. I got this." I took a big, deep breath. Then, I looked to my right, and out of the corner of my eye, I saw my friend Belinda. I thought to myself, "Something's not right with her. She's going to do something strange. I can tell." As I was watching Belinda, a tension started to build in the audience; they could see even more than I could. Before I realized what was happening, Belinda hit the floor like a ton of bricks and went into a deep crying wail, prostrate on the stage.

I was still thinking, "You got this. It's alright. Don't look at her."

So instead, I breathed and looked left, and I realized that there was trouble over there, too. At this point, there were three parents in the second row mimicking second position, trying to keep us focused on the dance routine instead of on Belinda. They were probably thinking, "Get your little ass into second position. I just spent $38 on hair and makeup and $32 on a damn tutu! Second position!"

Trouble on the left; disaster on the right. But I kept my cool, saying, "I got this. It's ok. Ignore them all!"

Trying to ignore Belinda and the parents, I looked around at my peers and realized that I was next to the chubby girl in the class. My mind raced, thinking, "She's the kind of kid that's going to take people out with her. I just know it." I can't remember her name but I remember that when she looked at me, I knew she could read my mind: "You come near me, and I'm going to push you off the stage. I am in second position. And I am wearing a shiny tutu. Don't you touch it!" I think I scared her, because she looked away very quickly. Then, before I knew it, she made a turn and grabbed another little girl's tutu, pulled her off stage—and they ran like hell. You know those types of people, the ones who think, "If I'm going down, I'm taking somebody with me." Do you have any of those people in your life? I knew from the moment that girl stood beside me that day that she was one of them.

Before I knew it, I was in the middle of a ballet recital war. It looked like we were on a battlefield, with soldiers in tutus scattered everywhere. Two moms in the third and fourth row were crying, with tears running down their cheeks. One was panicking, and one of the fathers was patting her arm. At that point, I realized that I better think of something. And this is my most vivid memory of that day: I looked down at my tiny feet in those little, white shoes. I took a big, deep breath and proceeded to break into the biggest tap dance you have ever seen.

I was just tapping and tapping. I tapped to the left until I hit one end of the stage, stepping over the ballet bodies. I just tap danced, back and forth, never stopping. This went on for a good seven minutes. By that point, my headpiece was off to one side, almost falling off my head completely. I was pouring sweat and my legs hurt. I was exhausted, so I decided to start walking and waving to give myself a breather. By now, the parents that had been crying were actually taking pictures, so, I stopped, smiled, and posed as they all laughed and clapped.

Then, the next terrifying thought came to mind. "How do I end something like this?" So, I was walking and waving and stepping over bodies, and, when I got to the middle of the stage, I made my big finish: a semi-well-done split, hands on my hips. The audience exploded in applause. I got up, took a bow, and walked off stage, telling the other dancers, on my way out, "Get up."

As soon as I got off stage, my mom, my dad, and Miss Anne were all standing and waiting for me. Then, the moment I got backstage, the tears just started streaming down my cheeks as I clasped my hands.

My dad asked, "Why are you crying?"

I quietly replied, "I was scared to death."

He said, "You didn't seem scared to death."

And I said, "No, I was!"

He said, "Honey, what just happened? If you were so scared to death, you didn't have to do it."

And I said, "I did have to do it."

He said, "Why?"

I said, "I had promised."

He took me, gave me a big hug and said, "That's commitment."

Then, Miss Anne leaned over and said, "That is Suzanne. I know you did it because you promised. But can I ask you a question? Why a tap dance?"

My answer: "It was just better than ballet. The audience was so sad. I wanted them to smile."

It takes guts to be extraordinary. I fully believe I had a lot more guts back when I was four years old than I do now. As we grow up and become adults, we just worry more—about how we will look, what people will think, and who we will offend.

At that dance recital, my only focus was to be extraordinary. That was all I wanted—and not someone else's version of extraordinary, but mine. I was less worried about the kids to the left and right and more concerned about the audience. That day, those people were my customers, and I wanted to make them happy.

Business takes guts. It requires that you be willing to be extraordinary, even when you have no clue if anyone will support you. Paying attention to every detail of my life left me lonely at times, but you have to be willing to be a little lonely, since it's the only way to truly focus on yourself. You have to fully commit to do and be whatever it takes to be successful. And the first step is doing what no one else is willing to do.

If the way you do anything is the way you do everything, consider your performance strategy. In other words, how do you know, without fail, that you have put in enough time and sweat to be extraordinary? Great basketball players shoot thousands of shots in dark gymnasiums when other kids go out to party. Great pastors read the Bible and revise their sermons while other people go home early. Legendary musicians play the same scales over and over while others catch up on their sleep. At what point do they decide *that's good enough*? Do they ever?

• • •

The film company describes the documentary *Jiro Dreams of Sushi* as "The story of 85-year-old Jiro Ono, considered by many to be the world's greatest sushi chef. He is the proprietor of Sukiyabashi Jiro, a ten-seat, sushi-only restaurant inauspiciously located in a Tokyo subway station. Despite its humble appearances, it is the first restaurant of its kind to be awarded a prestigious three-star Michelin Guide rating, and sushi lovers from around the globe make the pilgrimage to this spot, calling months in advance and shelling out top dollar for a coveted seat at Jiro's sushi bar."

Many people would call Jiro talented, gifted, or passionate, but Jiro himself has a simpler explanation. He says:

Once you decide on your occupation, you must immerse yourself in and fall in love with your work.... Never complain about your job. You must dedicate your life to mastering your skill. That's the secret of success, and is the key to being regarded honorably.

SUCCESS TAKES IMMERSION

I remember the summer 2008 Olympics in Beijing when swimmer Michael Phelps did something *never* done before. He became a legend, and I wondered how much he had endured in the years leading up to his record-breaking performance:

- How many early morning swims?
- How many pulled muscles?
- How many wins?
- How many losses?
- How much money had he saved?
- How much money had he spent?
- How many heartbreaks had he experienced?
- How many days did he have, days when he felt like he couldn't go on?
- Were there days when he knew he could do it?

In his 2004 autobiography *Beneath the Surface*, Phelps explains:

There are times in my sleep when I literally dream my race from start to finish. Other nights…I visualize to the point that I know exactly what I want to do: dive, glide, stroke, flip, reach the wall, hit the split time to the hundredth, then swim back again for as many times as I need to finish the race. [p. 23]

It's amazing when you consider what goes into winning an Olympic gold medal. What does it take? Some of it, like hard work, commitment, and dedication, is obvious. But there's something that isn't so obvious, and that's willpower.

- To find out what you really want for your life and business, you have to ask yourself what you are willing to sacrifice, to do, to be, and to try. How *willing* are you to fail?

14

- How *willing* are you to try something new?
- How *willing* are you to leave others behind so you can grow?
- How *willing* are you to get up again?
- What are you *willing* to start doing?
- What are you *willing* to stop doing?

For the first three years of growing my business, I kept a hand-made sign on my desk that read: THERE ARE NO CINDERELLA STORIES. And there aren't.

Will must be the entrepreneur's highest value. Are you playing to win or are you just hoping to stay in the race?

What are you willing to do *today* to dramatically stretch you toward your goals? What is your version of a legend? When you close your eyes, what do you see?

Chapter 1 Homework

That's right: There's homework at the end of every chapter.

What, you think you just get to sit here and read? My clients know that I expect them to work. I tell them every day, "This shit is hard; that's why it works."

I know we're only a few pages in, but I'm asking you to change up your game. It's why at the end of each chapter I'm going to ask you the big questions you need to consider if you're ready to make that change. Each question is strongly connected to the material I've written about, and while they may seem small or inconsequential, the truth is they'll give you a hell of a lot of insight into your character and how you show up in life.

If you're the type of person who skips over the exercises and says, "That's not for me," then you might as well throw this book out, because the odds are, you're skipping over the other hard work that's going to make a difference.

(continued)

(*continued*)

So, you can do things as you've always done and keep getting what you've already got, or you can pay attention to the questions I'm going to ask and start creating some new results.

The truth is it doesn't matter much to me either way, but for you, well, that's a totally different story. This chapter described a few things to keep in mind as you work to transition yourself and your business.

1. **Beware those who want to pull you down with them.** We all have people in our lives who are determined to take us down the rabbit hole. They are the ones who are too scared to try, or want to quit halfway through, and they don't want to do it alone.

   Who in your life wants to take you down when they feel like quitting? Go on, list them. (Don't worry; we won't tell them.)

2. **Commitment to oneself is the cornerstone of success.** If you don't believe what you promise, there's no way anyone else will either.

   Where have you made commitments for your clients, loved ones, and even yourself when you failed to follow through?

   What did that cost you personally and professionally?

   How might things have been different had you seen your promise through?

3. **It takes guts to be extraordinary.** I've already shared with you that I had a hell of a lot more guts at age four than I do now (and I'm a gutsy gal).

   Name your earliest memory of doing something extraordinary. Tell the story. What was going on in your life and in the moment? Spell it all out. Bring to mind the drama and the detail. Who was with you and why did you decide to step up and be better than you ever had before?

Now ask yourself what's changed since then? Why aren't you willing to take those steps again? What's holding you back? What excuses are standing in the way?

4. **Success is lonely.** Those who are truly successful are willing to do the things that others simply aren't.

What's the one thing in your life that no one else is willing to do?

How different would your life be if you took those extra steps and did the things others wouldn't?

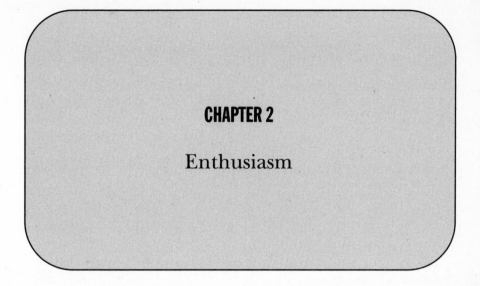

CHAPTER 2

Enthusiasm

I play to win, whether during practice or a real game. And I will not let anything get in the way of me and my competitive enthusiasm to win.

—Michael Jordan

I am standing on stage at an event in front of hundreds of people, with several of my clients in the audience. I am to give success tips and advice, and share my own rocky, hero's path. As the moderator opens up the audience to questions, one of my clients progresses to the microphone stand with quite a hop in her step. She states her name, her business, and tilts her head as she begins her question, which feels like it takes 45 minutes, but only really takes 45 seconds. She asks, "Suzanne, I've been working with you for two years on my business. Yet I still seem to be floundering, not making money, and am really unclear on my message. I am wondering if anyone on the panel has any suggestions?"

I swear I heard a death bell in both of my ears and the room fell silent. Some kind and gentle panelist handled the question very well, respected me, and moved on.

I was mortified. Every button I possessed was pushed. It felt like my eyes were blinking red and smoke was puffing from my ears like a Saturday-morning cartoon character. I managed to make my way off stage after the session and promptly began ruminating about it for a few days. I blamed that client, made myself feel bad, and even thought (just for a while) that I must be wrong or simply not good at what I do for a living. What did I do to her to make her feel as though she needed to say that—and, in public, in front of my other clients and peers?

Do you have someone in your life that pushes your buttons? Maybe a family member that says things that feel like a knife through your heart every time you speak of your business? These people somehow know what just to say and how to say it to ensure your day goes to hell from there. And it doesn't just ruin part of your well-planned business day; it puts a cloud over the whole damn day. Or week. Or sometimes even month.

I was crushed on the stage that day. The next day, I received an email from another client who'd been there to see me speak that same day. She witnessed how hard I'd taken that blow, and she had some advice for me. Her email simply read: "Suzanne, disconnect your wiring!"

What a lightbulb moment. We can't stop other people from saying things to us. We can't control others, but we can control our wiring, the voltage and the power we choose to give to a person or situation. I don't have to provide energy to that which does not serve me. I don't have to let another colleague, friend, or even partner impact my enthusiasm.

So think about it. What are you giving energy to? Are other people pushing buttons that you're letting impact your entire outlook?

Remember: *You* control your wiring. You can plug into negativity and disappointment, or you can plug into enthusiasm. It's up to you. As nineteenth-century philosopher Elbert Hubbard wrote, "Positive anything is better than negative nothing." What does this mean for you?

I first heard the term EBM a few years ago. It stands for emotional business management, and it is deadly.

It is an enthusiasm killer for the launching entrepreneur. All business owners will have ups and downs and highs and lows in business. There is always quite a bit of emotional energy swirling. You have a success, a client leaves, you get a joint venture, you endure some personal hiccups, you get an email from an unhappy customer, you go to an amazing seminar, and so on. Nothing is constant; there are peaks and valleys, and sometimes the income reflects these highs and lows as well.

You truly have to manage your emotional energy. It is the most important resource in your business. You need it to acquire clients, manage staff, and manifest your company's vision.

I have a simple strategy as to exactly where to put my emotional energy. I ask, "On my deathbed, how much will this matter, if at all?" Ninety percent of things will not matter at all, and I let them go, but 10 percent of the time I think, "Hmm, that would matter." That 10 percent is where I let my attention—and thus my enthusiasm—go.

It has kept most things very simple for me over the years and has kept me out of really vicious EBM.

I can't please everyone, be everything, and get it all right. No one can. BUT I can manage my energy to help those who want help and make differences where I can—and you can, too. You can't be in business to make friends, or to be liked all the time. You have to be clear that your enthusiasm steers the ship. Then the staff, the clients, and the money just follow your energy.

How are you managing your emotional energy? How is it affecting your business, clients, or life?

I can't thank my client enough for coaching me that day via email. While it certainly wasn't an enjoyable experience, I am also grateful for the client that came to the microphone and humiliated me. It was a life-long lesson in enthusiasm's fuel: resilience.

Passion is crucial, but it is simply not enough in the game of business. I see passion break the bank for one business owner after another. You have to have enthusiasm and enough resilience so that you can still find the energy to keep going when things go south.

What are you enthusiastic about? What is something you love to do so much that you would do it for free? What can you focus on as if nothing else exists? Find that. And when you find it, embrace it. Let it guide your decisions. You will never make a bad decision by following enthusiasm.

Passion is about emotion and feeling—and for that reason, it can trip you up. Enthusiasm is a little more useful, since it's about acting and reacting. It allows you to make thoughtful decisions and take the right action when things are going well. It also guides your reaction when things are going badly.

Whether I am writing my blog, this book, or being interviewed, I use these two questions to find enthusiasm:

1. What breaks my heart?
2. What pisses me off?

These days, a lot of books and a lot of talk focus on not having a job, escaping the corporate world, and finding the freedom of your own business. Don't get me wrong; I agree. I think entrepreneurship is the way to build your ultimate lifestyle and your ultimate legacy. It is why we are all in this. But there is a point where things go wrong. I talk to people and they say, "I want to build a business and not have a job. I don't want to go back to corporate, so I have to build my business." That conclusion is unfortunately ass-backwards. You don't build a business because you don't want a job. You don't build a business because you can't and don't want to go back to corporate. You don't build a business because you want freedom. You build a business because you have an idea that you are so enthusiastic about you have to build it.

The goal of building a business isn't to not have a job. In fact, it's quite the opposite. It's about making your job your entire life—and having so much enthusiasm that you would work two jobs to make it happen. Whenever I discuss this topic, I can't stop thinking about the following quote from rapper P. Diddy: "Don't chase the paper; chase the dream."

Most business consultants will tell you not to chase anything. You simply have to create marketing and messaging that attracts followers, and they'll naturally come to you. While I agree with this, I think P. Diddy was on to something. I know firsthand that you have to chase something while growing a business and turning a profit day in and day out. I know that money always follows dedication. So often, people tell me they are working toward their passion, but not making any money. Passion is essential, but it only gets you started. Enthusiasm keeps you going.

What I am about to tell you is the real secret to success. Yes, I will admit it. If you only get this one thing, you could stop reading here. *The key to success is to be the last one standing.*

Most other people will quit because their passions change, or the fight gets too hard. If you truly believe in your work, you do not give up, give in, or stop. Ever. You find the enthusiasm every single day.

If you are chasing your dream, the money will follow as a result. If I hear one more time that I have been able to do what I have done because of my subject or luck or angle or hair color or whatever, I will just scream. Give me a break! I did it because I decided that failure was not an option.

I chose to be enthusiastic about it all—even the total disasters. I probably should have kept a list somewhere of all my failed programs, because there have been many. At one time, I was launching more losers than winners, but regardless of success or failure, I focused on the process, the journey, and how I showed up throughout. When you become unconsciously or consciously attached to the outcome, you begin putting your own needs over those of your clients and customers. And that's when you start to falter—because people buy to solve their problems, not yours.

I was just working with a client this morning, and asked her to answer the following question about her strategy and planning: What would this launch look like if I did not do it out of a need for money?

Play this game with me for a moment, and imagine that the money is all gone. Suppose that you will *never* make a dime doing what you are currently doing. Would you still do it?

Okay, you might be a total idiot if you said yes, and only yes. But you might be a business genius if you said, "Yes, but I will find a way to make money doing it." THAT is enthusiasm. Chase that dream.

Chapter 2 Homework

Okay, let's talk about enthusiasm.

1. **Negativity is the enemy of enthusiasm.** When you focus on what's wrong all the time, you don't have the space to be enthusiastic.

(continued)

(*continued*)

How are you letting negativity hurt your ability to be enthusiastic?

Whose negativity are you letting affect your mood?

2. **Let's talk about emotional business management (EBM).**

Can you name three instances when you employed EBM in a decision or interaction in your life or business?

Did they help or hurt your business?

What would have happened had you been able to disconnect your wiring and think clearly?

3. **The 90/10 principle.** Think about everything you have on your plate right now.

How much of it is *truly* important?

If you were on your deathbed, how much of your struggles will really have been important over your lifetime?

What are the 10 percent of things in your life that are important to you?

What about the 90 percent of the things that don't matter? Is it time to let go?

4. **Resilience is enthusiasm's fuel.**

What does resilience mean to you?

When was the last time in your life you were truly resilient?

Where could a little resiliency do a little good in your world?

5. **On the subject of enthusiasm:**

Where could you use a little enthusiasm in your world right now?

Where is focusing too much on passion hurting you?

6. **Why the hell are you here?**

   Why are you in business?

   Why did you spend $22 to learn about business from me?

   Most importantly, what are you so enthusiastic about creating that you're willing to take the lonely road of entrepreneurship to bring it to life?

7. **Be the last one standing.** Think about a time when you were the last one standing.

   What was going on?

   Why did you choose to stand when everyone else fell or quit? What was so important to you that you refused to stop?

   Do you have that same commitment to your business and life?

   How far are you willing to go? How much frustration, stress, failure, and fights are you willing to endure?

8. **Enthusiasm in failure and in success.**

   Name your last two successes. What did they teach you?

   Now name your last two failures. What did they teach you?

   Which do you think had more value? (Hint: If you learned more from your successes, you're doing something wrong.)

CHAPTER 3

Commitment

In any moment of decision, the best thing you can do is the right thing, the next best thing is the wrong thing, and the worst thing you can do is nothing.
—Theodore Roosevelt

Most of us have been hearing most of our lives about how special we are. But the unfortunate truth is, you just aren't that special.

I know. Take it in. Swallow hard. It's a reality check. We have been told forever that we were special. Our parents said so. Our participation trophies said so.

We know we are born into specialness and have something huge to offer the world, but a curious thing happens to a lot of people: We decide we are different, and not in a good way. We're different in that we just can't do it for one reason or another. We feel that we *need* to be different or this whole life and business thing might be way too easy. When we adopt a defeatist mindset, we deeply believe that we must be different. We have special circumstances, so we can't make more money or get more clients because we are different, or lesser, somehow. We aren't good enough.

Let me provide a short list of some of the reasons you might be different:

- Health issues
- Debt
- Family problems
- Relationship challenges
- A day job
- A set of made-up rules we have created for ourselves
- No car
- No hair
- No clean underwear

Chances are you don't have that many problems. But what are the odds that most people don't have at least one problem on that list, or countless others?

Pity is gratification for losers. Problems don't make you different; they make you the same as everyone else who has problems. And every single one of us does, in one way or another. What makes us different is how we overcome them.

31

One of my clients told me the funniest story a couple of weeks ago. She said she wasn't going to go hiking because it looked like rain. It wasn't raining, and it might not. But there was a possibility for rain, so she decided not to do what she'd originally planned because of the very small chance that something might go wrong.

A friend contemplating parenthood was agonizing over the possibility that her child would be born with some sort of medical problem. She worried about being sick herself during pregnancy, the child having ADHD (which I attempted to soothe her about by telling her that it has served me really well), or things not being perfect in some way. She decided too much could go wrong, so she shouldn't have a child. There were no signs of any impending issues; but there was a chance for something to go terribly, terribly, terribly wrong.

Guess what? It could rain. My friend's child could have problems. It could all go wrong.

We spend most of our lives doing this. We stop, slow down, and complain because it *might* rain. Our plans might get messed up. Our goals might not work out. But, then again, they just might.

Commitment is simply the ability to do something and avoid doing nothing at all costs. I have had people tell me throughout my entire life that I overwhelm them; I decide too fast, and they are trying to catch up. I certainly don't try to do this, but I will say: I have no regrets. This is how I approach life, and it's worked out well for me. I have made tons of mistakes, but I have no regrets.

You can't commit to anything until you decide to do something, take an action, or make a move. The following explanation appeared in the March 2005 *Journal of Neuroscience* report "Decision Making in Leeches":

> *Animals react to changes [in] the environment by responding with an appropriate behavior (from simple escape responses in invertebrates, to decision strategies in primates).*

In other words, animals react quickly, much more so than humans. If you have a family pet, watch it. Animals never stay in indecision. Scared? They fight or flee. Excited? They approach or steal. Nervous?

They retreat or submit. Animals have this all figured out. It's simple: Do something. Commit. Apparently, even leeches are more committed than most people.

The truth is we are all different. And it's entirely true that some of us have good luck, while others have been dealt a shitty hand. However, no one is singled out for evil or failure or hard times. We create those. We look outside and say it *might* rain.

In *Your Money Puzzle: Piecing Together Your Financial Security*, American actor Clayton Moore, famous for portraying the Lone Ranger, says:

> Most people think that making decisions is hard, especially financial decisions, so they end up burying their heads in the sand, hoping someone else will make their decisions for them. The thing to realize is that by not making decisions, we are really making decisions anyway. We are really deciding that we will continue to do what we have done up until now. [p. 226]

So whatever you do or fail to do next is a decision either way. The latter simply renders you completely out of control, while the former empowers you to commit to the next idea, client, or step in the plan.

Getting caught in this trap is, quite simply, just an excuse, nothing more. Failing to commit without someone else's assistance is just crap. I hear it all the time. The husband, kids, boss, or business partner needs to be in on this. It's just another line on your list of reasons you are "different." It's also an easy out. That lizard brain kicks in and reminds you it *could* rain, and you are relieved to know someone else can help you in making another bad decision or no decision at all.

Commitment is only about you.

I love watching and hearing from folks in January: the grand month of renewal and resolutions. I like to watch people floundering to change, be better, and promise to be different, you know, the same New Year BS we all put ourselves through.

To put it bluntly: It will be a new year, but it will still be an old you. There is nothing you need to become or morph into. There is no magic New Year's pill that will make your business more profitable or your sales soar. You just need to pay attention to the right things.

So, what are you paying attention to? Is it what's going to help you achieve your goals and live and grow your business?

I received a great card from someone recently that provided some very valuable guidance on how to start paying attention to your commitment and those around you:

I only listen and play with the winners…those that know what they want, know where they are going, and do it in prosperity and joy!

Commitment has to be deliberate. It has to do with who you're surrounding yourself with, and what your collective focus is. This will ultimately set your navigation system on auto-pilot.

So ask yourself:

- Is where you're headed right now where you want to go?
- What products or services do you make or offer?
- Are you proud of them?
- How does your sales team represent you?

We hold events with thousands of folks in attendance, and the details are deadly. Even after years of speaking, I walk into the room and I see the placement of every chair, how it is positioned, and where it goes. I look at every detail before we open the doors.

If you are going to be committed to business, you have to be committed to your clients, their every experience, and what it takes to make their experience exceptional.

You must first decide. Then commit. Then, and only then, do you succeed.

Chapter 3 Homework

1. The need to be special.

How has the need to be special sabotaged your success?
How has it affected the way you treat others or expect to be treated?

What would happen if no one thought you were special? Would you care? How would it affect the way you showed up in life?

2. **Let's talk about your problems.** Consider this your one-time pass. I want you to take a moment and list out all your problems. C'mon, this is your chance to create that gripe list.

Do your problems make you feel special?

Do you think other people think they make you feel special?

Are you using them as an excuse?

What would happen if you overcame those problems? Would that make you special?

3. **Obstacles.** We've all got them.

What three obstacles are standing in the way of you making more money, having more fun, feeling better about yourself?

What have you done about them lately?

What's the one action you could take *right now* that would make a difference? Now go do it. I'm dead serious. Go. If you don't, I'll know.

4. **No decision is a decision.** Name the last big decision you avoided.

Did sticking your head in the sand help or hurt you?

What might have happened if you actually made that decision instead of doing nothing?

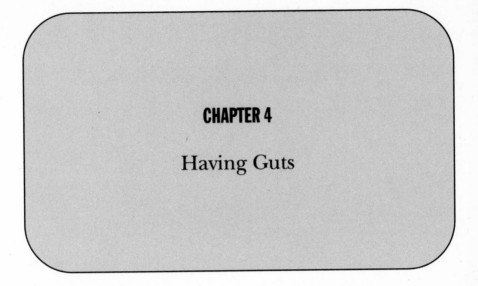

CHAPTER 4

Having Guts

I'm going to work so that it's a pure guts race at the end, and if it is, I am the only one who can win it.

—Steve Prefontaine

The phrase we all know is *not* "believing is seeing," but rather "seeing is believing!"

"Seeing is believing," my friend, is pure raw guts. All the marketing, ass kicking, love, support, cheerleading, and strategy in the world will be useless if you do not know what you want. It is as simple as going and getting it.

A friend told me that as much as she wanted to bow out of a difficult situation, she had to stay involved because it provided "security." Sorry, that's an *excuse*. And I just don't accept excuses!

The following is a list of my least favorite excuses. Chances are that at least one of these will hit home for you, and possibly even piss you off. If it does, well, get in line.

"I can't make a change because of..."

1. Money
2. My kids
3. My weight
4. My spouse
5. My skills
6. My education
7. My fear
8. Time

I know an overweight woman who was overwhelmed with the commitments of her three kids and a 60-hour-a-week job. She was living paycheck to paycheck, and even got an eviction notice at one point. Though she had an education, it wasn't in an area that interested her or helped her do what she wanted to do with her life, and the job she was in had actually caused the quality of her skills to suffer.

She was scared to death. Paralyzed. She actually found herself on the subway having a panic attack and almost passed out. She felt trapped. During a walk around the block later that night, she burst into tears, and came to the realization that if she was going to live out her dreams, she had to make four decisions:

1. To make a plan and not worry (yet) about exactly how to carry it out.
2. To tell the scared side of her to shut the hell up—on a daily basis.
3. To be willing to look like a fool.
4. To not make or accept excuses.

So, I may be fat. I may occasionally look like a fool. And I definitely get scared sometimes. But the reality is that guts make it work. I deal with those four things every day and I use them to guide my decisions. I have learned that guts can trump smarts and experience.

Pony up, people; we only get one ride. And the only way to change *your* world is to make one (gutsy) decision at a time.

I'm going to let you in on one of my little secrets: When I don't know it, don't have it, or can't find it, I make it up. I generate it. I create it. You're probably wondering what the *it* is.

When I say "make it up," I don't mean offering misleading information or failing to tell the truth. I am simply talking about utilizing resources and getting away from the I-don't-know syndrome.

You have to create your answers; they aren't always just there. When you have a goal in mind, there is no such thing as "I don't know" or "maybe." That just does not work with the universe; these concepts are manmade. I have eliminated those terms from my vocabulary and world, and I challenge other people to do the same. When people say they don't know, I tell them they do. It annoys them sometimes; but it does give them a little jolt, and makes them consider what their truth is. Do they really not know? Or is the answer simply something they don't want to consider?

"I don't know where I will get the money." Yes you do. You might have to make a sacrifice to get it, but you know. Get some guts and decide to make that sacrifice.

40

"*Maybe I will try this approach.*" If you're not certain about it, then don't. *Maybe* is a no-go. As Yoda so wisely pointed out, "Do or do not; there is no try." Get some guts.

"*I don't know how to do it.*" Then ask someone who does. Get some guts.

We always know deep down what it takes but are often driven to inaction by fear. And this fear manifests itself as excuses.

Save yourself time, energy, money, and frustration—and stop fooling yourself. "I don't know" is a game you have chosen to play that allows you to remain stagnant. It is safe, and your family, friends, and colleagues have made it socially acceptable. They don't necessarily mean to, but they enable your apathy and fear. So move on. Let go of the beliefs that hold you back and make you doubt yourself, and surround yourself with success, one gutsy decision at a time. You can try to avoid and look outside yourself, but at some point you have to muster the guts to go through it because that's the only way to get unstuck.

Whether it's overcoming through failure, having to let a team member go, investing another $100,000 or $100,000,000 in your business, or launching your latest program, you have a way to get from where you are to where you need to be. What I mean is, the only way to figure it out, get smarter, get better, or find out what actually works is to go through the experience.

I'll put it in context: Somewhere between the organic tomatoes and bananas at our local Whole Foods, I started my business. I draped a simple folding table with some poorly cut blue fabric from Wal-Mart. I was armed with 100 poorly printed business cards and a sign with my logo printed on it from Staples. It was where our friends and neighbors shopped, and I had convinced the manager to let me set up a little table on Sundays. I was standing in the produce department, asking people who passed by if they would like to discuss life coaching.

It took guts.

My friends thought I was a little nuts and my partner wouldn't shop at the store while I was manning my booth. I was even a little embarrassed myself at times; but that feeling gave me the motivation to keep going. I figured if I had the guts to stand there and offer my services to complete strangers, then eventually someone would have the guts to become a client. And they did. It didn't happen overnight, and it wasn't easy, but it happened.

I wish there was a magic pill for guts because you can't be in business without them. In fact, there's very little you can do in life that's worthwhile if you can't muster up a bit of courage. There are no magic pills of course, which I actually believe is a blessing in disguise. If you don't have the guts to put yourself out there, the lessons would be lost. The insights would be worthless. The most important thing we can give ourselves in our business is some guts. The only way out is through. If you take a look at businesses that succeed, you'll notice that every single one of them took guts to create, grow, and flourish.

So yes....

You have to make the phone calls.

You have to keep investing.

You have to learn the lessons.

You have to care about your dream more than anyone.

You have to have tenacity.

You have to do the work.

You have to stand by your decisions, and be your own biggest cheerleader.

You have to stop waiting for someone else to give you permission to go after your dreams.

The only way out is through. If you aren't doing the scary stuff in this moment, then you aren't making the money you could make or growing the business at the speed you could grow it.

Be honest for a moment. What is your biggest struggle right now? What is the action or step that is just too scary for you to take? What is your "got to get some guts" moment that you can actually feel physically? It is likely your biggest business challenge.

Maybe it is:

- Making money
- Losing money
- A spouse
- A child
- Your weight
- Your health
- Your environment
- A difficult choice

Whatever your burden is, focus on it. No matter how painful or seemingly unfair, zero in.

Ask yourself how bad you *really* want the thing this obstacle is keeping you from getting. It's not going to get less scary or easier; in fact, the longer you wait, the scarier it gets.

When you do the gutsy things in business, it always pays off. When you do your best, people notice. Here's a confession that might not surprise you much: I like attention, and I noticed early in life when you do your best, when you go beyond 100 percent and are full of guts, people notice. When people notice, you get attention. When you get attention, you get leverage. And leverage, my friends, is extremely powerful.

I have always tried to close my eyes and take the plunge, even— perhaps especially—when a situation is not certain or safe. I can frustrate staff (even spouses) in my tenacity to do something over and over in order to get it right. I typically outwork my team, which guarantees one very important thing: When I do my best, everyone around me wants to do their best. When I take risks, others want to take risks.

Taking risks while doing your best is money in the bank. And doing your best shows up in many ways:

- Physical
- Mental
- Time
- Ethic
- Value
- Giving back
- Creatively
- Teamwork
- Courage

Do you have the guts to sacrifice some security? I am certain I chose this life, this path, and this world; it wasn't handed to me. With that choice comes responsibility to do my best so others can be their best.

Are you doing your best? Are you taking risks?

I'll share something with you that I mean with as much sincerity as I can muster: If my business went belly up, I'd be ok. You know why? I still have that tablecloth and sign I used at Whole Foods. And I still have guts.

Chapter 4 Homework

1. **Excuses.** Look, we've all got them. And we use them as socially acceptable reasons to not reach our goals. Sure, you can get sympathy with a well-placed excuse at the foot of the right person, but excuses don't grow your business.

   So, why don't we just get yours out of the way, and we can move on from here?

2. **Got guts?** Then prove it.

Name the last time you showed true guts—the kind of guts that would impress even your harshest critic.

What happened in that situation? What made you show guts at that moment?

What was the payoff from both a business perspective and for your personally?

Now think about the last time you didn't show guts when you had an opportunity to shine and simply failed.

Why didn't you show up and put it all out there?

Where's that one place in your business that would make a huge difference if you just showed some serious guts?

3. **The only way out is through.**

What do you want to accomplish today? I'm serious.

What is your goal for this very moment?

Is it something you think you can get done?

A big obstacle you can accomplish?

Are you waiting for a sign from God before doing anything—waiting for permission or to be told what to do? Or is the only way to get this goal done is to get off your ass and get moving? Put another way: What do you need to do to "get through" to the other side?

4. **Spill your guts.**

How do *you* define guts?

How does having guts factor into the actions you take every day?

Where could you show a little more, and how would that impact your business?

(continued)

(*continued*)

5. Gut check time.

Are you a risk taker? Are you willing to take chances to grow your business and change your life?

What chances are you actually taking?

How far are you willing to go to bring your dream to life?

What are you willing to risk (and potentially lose) to have the chance of getting what you actually want?

CHAPTER 5

Being Embarrassed

"Do not be embarrassed by your failures, learn from them and start again."
—Richard Branson

I started my business like most people: confused but optimistic.

I read, listened, and learned as much as I could. There were days when I was so overwhelmed and confused that I essentially closed my eyes and chose one action item to do, wildly ignoring any sense of intelligent order.

Sometimes I did nothing, which is of course a big no-no. There was something a little dangerous and very frightening about asking people to work with me, because even though I was smart and capable, I wasn't totally clear on what the hell I was doing. I was willing but hesitant. I could feel it. I could talk about my business openly and freely with people I knew well, but froze up around people I didn't already know.

Obviously, I couldn't just talk about my business with friends. This approach was going to take forever; I knew I had to get over myself.

Riding the train from New Jersey to New York City isn't a very enjoyable task for most commuters; indeed, it's a necessary evil. However, this environment became my business lab. Because I worked 60 hours or more a week, I had to use every available minute of free time to launch my business.

Every morning, I would write a business to-do list that usually included items like this:

- Write an email to former colleagues.
- Call local Chamber of Commerce.
- Follow up with nice lady from networking event.

One day, out of nowhere, an item appeared on the list as though someone else had written it:

- Be willing to look like an ass.

I realized that up until that point, I hadn't been. I had been willing to work and learn, but not do whatever it took, even if that meant being embarrassed. I might be stubborn, but I'm a quick learner, and I had an important message for myself: "Suzanne, you have to be willing to fail. You have to be willing to look stupid. You just might—and in fact, you probably will—get embarrassed. And guess what? You have to get over it."

And that was a turning point.

Entrepreneurship can be crazy and overwhelming, especially when you're just starting out. Unless you are a software startup with $50 million in funding, you have to bootstrap—and bootstrapping can look, well, embarrassing. Take me, for example: with 100 business cards, $500 left on a credit card, and a dream. When this happens you have no choice but to go big, go wild, go strong, and possibly… maybe… *definitely* look like an ass.

• • •

At TechCrunch Disrupt in May 2013, big-time NYC seed-stage venture capital duo Ben and Ken Lerer shared their number-one tip for young entrepreneurs: "Be psychotic."

Ben jokingly claims that this was the number-one quality he looks for in an entrepreneur. But all kidding aside, the team does "focus far more on a founder's passion and drive than the actual product," says Ben. "We focus on people, not companies." When they've slipped up and allowed themselves to get more excited about a sector or product and put less emphasis on the person, the companies tended to not be their best performers in the portfolio.

The lesson? Your product won't do anything unless you are. So be the wildly passionate, committed, enthusiastic, and little bit crazy entrepreneur (with a plan!). You have to be just psychotic enough to fail.

• • •

One of my private clients is an anti-diet expert. She has been coaching people to abandon diets and embrace eating their own way for years; however, her practice has been a bit stop-and-go for a while, until recently.

We had been discussing her tentative plan to put together an anti-diet system (there was a big *maybe* around this plan). She had been playing with it a bit until one day, something felt different. She shifted personally, and when she shifted, everything changed. In the matter of just a few weeks, she developed a marketable system, a new website, an entire plan, and started generating cash. So, what shifted and led to her success? She decided to take a chance at *failing*. Yep! You heard me right. For better or worse, she was ready to put it all on the line, and she did it fearlessly! Only then was she able to start chasing after what she wanted, and that's how you've got to see it, too.

What are you willing to fail at in life, in business, in your career? What are you ready to put on the line? Are you ready to *decide* to just do it?

The defeat will feel constant at times, as will the shame. I remember thinking quite often, "I hope no one saw that!" You will launch programs that no one notices, and fail dreadfully at projects that launch but fall apart at some point down the line. Sometimes you will keep things on your to-do list for weeks…ok, even months, but the good thing about defeat is that it motivates you. It certainly has motivated me—because it reminds me that I am on the path and taking action. After all, you can't experience defeat if you're doing nothing. Every time I fail or miss the mark, I make certain to say one of two things:

1. "Wow. Fascinating. Too funny."
2. "Screw it. No need to figure this one out."

And then I move on.

There are times it can be exhausting, but that doesn't last for long. It's like that moment when you're running on the treadmill and you feel like you absolutely have to stop and get off, but you push yourself and then it seems kind of easy until the end. I believe they call it a "runner's groove." So stay in the game, and you will find your business groove.

RUN WITH THE LEAD DOGS

One of my early mentors always told me to run with the lead dogs. They are easy to find because they stand out.

While everyone else is comfortably sitting in the corner hoping to not be noticed, the lead dogs are on the verge of looking like jackasses while accomplishing big things. If you want to be innovative, be wealthy, and be known, then find that crowd.

Whatever situation you find yourself in, in whatever part of life—business, personal, career, relationships, hobby—you have to stick with the head of the pack to make a difference. It's a cliché, but it's true: It takes a village to build a business. Being part of a tribe makes you even more powerful, and helps you feel in total control of your undertakings.

Make sure you are surrounding yourself with people who are wiser, stronger, and more ambitious—and spend time with those people *every* day. It all starts by getting out of the house more—getting out of your old *life* more!

Learn fast that taking up less space and surrounding yourself with people who want to go unnoticed and stay under the radar won't get you more business, better clients, or cutting-edge marketing ideas. Success takes up space.

• • •

I want to get personal and ask you four important questions:

1. Why are you doing what you're doing in business?
2. Are you proud of what you do?
3. How many people do you tell daily about your business and the service you provide?
4. Are you willing to take risks and be seen?

I ask these questions because I want you to feel proud and excited, and to take up a little more space. When you do, you'll start to make more money. And money doesn't solve all of life's problems; it just magnifies people, and makes them more of who they truly are. If you're an asshole when you're broke, having money will only make you a bigger asshole. If you're a giving lover of life, having money will just amplify that.

What you are doing needs to be important enough for you to be working on it and trying to make it better. So go ahead. Take up more space. The world needs more of you in it. I need more of you in it. You'll get used to how it feels—and soon, you won't be embarrassed at all.

You'll just be wealthy.

Chapter 5 Homework

1. **To act or not to act?**

   What was the last bold yet blind action you took?
   How did it feel to do something without being sure whether it was the right thing to do?
   What happened as a result?
   Was it better than doing nothing?

2. **Look like an ass.**

   Are you willing to look like one?
   Can you name the last time you took a chance and looked like a big ol' silly horse's ass?
   Better yet, have you *ever* allowed yourself to look like one?
   If not, what might happen if you looked a little silly?

3. **Decide to fail.** Are you willing to fail? Don't just say yes because you think it sounds good; are you literally willing to fail?

   What would happen if you took your next big leap or launch knowing that you may very well fail completely?
   Would the universe collapse?
   Or would you simply get back on your feet and learn?

4. **Failure versus doing nothing.**

   Which is worse? Choose now.

   (continued)

(*continued*)

5. Your lead dogs.

What pack are you running with? List your five "lead dogs."

If you're not hanging out with them enough, how can you spend more time with them? (Please note: we do not advocate stalking.)

Why are these people good for you?

6. Your hind dogs.

Who are the dogs nipping at your feet that you need to get rid of?

Why have you tolerated them, and how much better off would you be if you let them go?

CHAPTER 6

Having Faith

Faith is believing in something when common sense tells you not to.
—Fred Gailey, *Miracle on 34th Street*

I'm standing in a hay field wondering how the hell I ended up here.

Well, I shouldn't be too dramatic. I do know how I got here. I paid to be here. Specifically, I had registered my amazing superhero dog, Lucky Boy, in a national tracking competition.

Tracking is a bit like search and rescue. The dog follows a scent track laid by humans to find a glove at the end. Truth be told, there are many moments in life when I wonder how the hell I got wherever I am, but on this day I am ready…ready to be the dope on the end of the rope.

The dog walks the course but the trainer is on the lead—and sometimes I feel I am there just to lose. The dog could probably run this thing flawlessly, but there is a catch: In order to succeed, you have to have faith in your dog. You have to trust he can follow the scent better than your rational, logical brain. I am sure you can see how this goes wrong quite often.

I cannot even tell you how much I have learned about my business and life by training my dogs. It's unbelievable.

Here's how a tracking test works:

A human lays a trail (simply by walking it) and drops their scent for about 500 yards, all while taking right and left turns, going over some obstacles, etc. The track ages for about an hour or two, then the dog is put on a lead and tracks the scent to the end, where there is a glove. It's unbelievable to watch!

The dog is the expert. It uses its nose and instincts to run the track. The track I was working on took the handler before me almost 45 minutes to run (successfully). That is a long time; most dogs run it in about 20 to 30 minutes max. It's a process that involves faith, and faith takes patience.

The handler *trusted* and *encouraged* her dog. She stood her ground. She didn't give up on her dog. She knew they both had the necessary skills to complete the task. She had the faith that most others don't have when working with dogs. The minute we get scared, our lizard brain tells us we know better than our own faith and instinct. It forces us to be logical because faith is not scientific, and logic is.

How are you handling your goals and life?

Are you solely focused on the glove at the end?

Are you trying to rush and force it all to happen?

Do you lose faith if you don't immediately get the result or answers that you want?

I stood in the middle of that field that day and thought, "This is what faith is all about." Life, business, work all require:

- Patience
- Trusting ourselves
- Standing our ground
- Never giving up
- Encouraging ourselves and those around us
- Knowing we are enough and that we have what it takes

When you learn to listen to yourself, and trust that the work you have done and the experience you have is enough to guide you, faith kicks in—and business gets a lot easier. You must use your intuition, whether it's taking on a client, making a business decision or even getting out of the car in a dark parking lot.

I have grown a fairly large team that includes legal experts for looking over contracts, accountants and bookkeepers for running numbers, COOs, and a CEO. There are many decisions that I now leave to people who know more than I do in one particular area. You have to have faith in yourself and your abilities, but it's just as crucial to have faith in other people.

Entrepreneurs are tricky manipulators. They tend to tell themselves no one is as smart, capable, or caring as they are. As a result, they get stuck suffering from *"founder syndrome"*: They can't do it alone, but they don't have enough faith in others to do it.

Faith in others is the ultimate way to run your business—unless your intuition says something different. You have to have faith in yourself above others. Faith in yourself allows you to trust your support team, which you need to grow. But sometimes *you* are your best team member, consultant, and adviser. You know your business because you *are* your business.

Every time I didn't follow my intuition, I have regretted it. You can let what seems like a simple decision slide—even when you have faith that you know the right thing to do—and it can end up becoming a big mess. You know when you know better. And while everything happens for a reason, faith is about having the ability and confidence to center yourself. It requires you to follow your instincts, pause, reflect, listen to your gut, and come from what you know—and to regularly ask yourself questions like the following:

- How often do you ignore your intuition in your marketing and business?
- Might you need to hire a new assistant?
- Are you certain you need to be speaking?
- Is your gut telling you to slow down, write that book, and launch it?
- Does the marketing you're currently using feel icky and need tweaking?

If you don't follow your gut, then you don't have a business crisis; you have a faith crisis. Most people think they must gather more knowledge before they can commit. They're convinced that logic must rule, and they want the absolute answer. The how is what stops 90 percent of people. They want to know more, be more, train more, plan more before they leap. But leaping prior to knowing is always your best bet. You have to be okay with failure, mistakes, and mishaps. In fact, you have to embrace them.

Business is messy. When things get to be too much, I suggest you close your eyes and keep going. Faith is powerful. Take it from the ultimate eye-closer: It will get you through!

● ● ●

Inspirational author Mike Dooley, who puts out a daily newsletter entitled "Notes from the Universe," sent the following amazing and eye-opening reminder a few years ago:

> *Yesterday I watched a small bird, flying very fast, disappear into the canopy of an oak tree. So dense were its leaves that it was impossible to see what happened next, though I can tell you it remained inside.*
>
> *I wondered how the little bird found its opening through the leaves at such a speed, and then managed to gently align its fragile body on the branch it chose to land upon, all within a fraction of a second. Not to mention the impossible-to-imagine flying maneuvers required: the banking, the curling, the vertical and horizontal stabilizations, the deceleration and landing.*
>
> *Memory? Calculation? Not in that tiny brain. Instinct? Maybe, but how does instinct know which way the branches of a tree have grown when no two are the same?*
>
> *Suzanne, that little bird just knew. It had faith, despite not being able to see how things would work out, that if (and only if) it stayed the course, the details would be taken care of; that an opening would appear and a twig would be found. In fact, had she slowed down enough to carefully and logically inspect the tree first, the prudent thing to do, she would have lost her lift and fallen to the ground.*
>
> *[It's] kind of like reaching for your dreams. Neither memory, nor calculating, nor instincts are the deciding factors, but faith coupled with action.*[1]

I invite you to stop white-knuckling and worrying about being all-knowing for a while. Surrender to faith. The moment you fail or fear, you start forcing it *big time.* You start overworking, pushing, and convincing people, instead making your business a customer-based service.

I know because I've been there and I've done that. And one thing I have learned about going from secretary to seven figures is that when you surrender to faith, you find flow.

I remember very specifically trying to fill a certain program, just pushing and pushing and getting very little result. I then thought, *just surrender.* Stop forcing this; instead, become aware of other

---

[1]©Mike Dooley, www.tut.com

opportunities. My single-minded focus on that one project was causing me to miss out on the other chances surrounding me. And wouldn't you know it, the second I stopped obsessing, an amazing (big-ticket) client came into my life. That client was a lot more fun than the program I'd been agonizing over—and working with her was a better ROI for the business.

So often we get fixed on HOW the money is coming in, and it blinds us to other opportunities. Be aware, and consider what Napoleon Hill advises in his book *Think and Grow Rich*: "Usually the money and opportunity will appear in the form of temporary defeat." That's not luck or coincidence. That is faith.

Let me say it again (just for good measure): It's not about *luck*. It's about *faith*.

How much faith do you have in this moment? Not just necessarily in yourself or your business, but just faith in general? If you feel that it's lacking, consider that sometimes it's just hidden—and you might be surprised at the little places where faith can jump out. Consider that:

- When we get on a plane, we have *faith* it is going to fly.
- When we go to bed, we have *faith* that in the morning there will be light.
- When we leave our house, we have *faith* that it will be there when we return.

When you look at it that way, you realize that 90 percent of our daily activities are solely based on our faith and belief. Without faith, we wouldn't even be able to get out of bed in the morning.

Faith fuels our very being. Yet it seems to be in short supply when it comes to getting clients and building our business. If we hold a workshop and one person shows, then we tell ourselves we have the wrong niche. If the first 10 people we ask say no to our service, we convince ourselves that we have awful marketing. Where is the faith?

• • •

A good friend shared this wonderful analogy with me this weekend about business building: If I'm handed 10,000 oysters and told 10 contain a million-dollar pearl, I begin to open them. *Phew.* Oysters are hard to open. One, two, three, four, and still no pearl. Shoot. Five, six. Ouch! I cut my hand. This really is hard. Seven, eight, nine, ten. Still no pearl. So frustrating. This is a stupid idea. There are no pearls in any of these. I hate oysters. I don't even want a million dollars.

Then, before you know it, the faith is gone.

Faith is tested when things get hard, when we are afraid, and when our perfectly laid plans don't work out so perfectly, but faith doesn't depend on things going as planned. True faith is continued belief in the face of adversity. It's what you know you have when you have every single reason in the world to have *no* faith, especially in business. And it is in these moments that you need to hold on to it most tightly.

Here's how:

1. **Be clear about what you want.** Faith wavers when it is uncertain about what to claim. So claim what you want.
2. **Stop being realistic.** The magic happens when you're unreasonable.
3. **Stop looking for the results.** The second you stop obsessively seeking them, they will come. Your job is to have faith, take action, and repeat.
4. **Know that our faith will be constantly tested.** You pass the test when you continue to believe. As the saying goes, "Faith isn't faith until it's all you're holding on to."

No business was ever built on uncertainty, and no leader every magically appeared out of doubt.

Faith is a full-time job. Day one on the job is to surrender. Don't be surprised if most financial success comes from the most unlikely places. That's just your paycheck from the job of faith.

Chapter 6 Homework

1. Faith versus logic.

Are you practicing enough faith-based action?

Does your logical side short-circuit your faith muscle?

Have you ever started an action based on faith, and then stopped because your logical side told you it was crazy? How did that work out for you?

2. Faith is all about trust.

Do you trust yourself?

Do you believe you have what it takes to be successful?

Do you have faith that you know best, and that there's no need to overanalyze?

Do you have faith in other people?

When was the last time you let go of your need to control and just trusted someone else to support you?

3. What's your I.Q. (intuition quotient)?

Do you listen to your intuition?

When was the last time you ignored it? What was the situation? How did it come back to haunt you?

When was the last time your intuition told you one thing, and the rest of the world told you another? Who did you listen to, and who was right in the end?

4. Planning to plan.

Are you someone who suffers from analysis paralysis?

Do you try to qualify everything or do you just go for it?

(Once again), are you okay with failing?

5. Surrender to faith.

Where in your business or life are you "forcing the issue"?

Where could a little extra faith help?

(continued)

(continued)

When was the last time you acted solely on instinct?

What might happen for you if you tried that a little bit more?

6. Right in front of your nose.

What opportunities might be right in front of your nose that you're missing because you're trying just a bit too hard? List a few that you know you missed because you were so focused on one thing and didn't see the other right in front of you.

7. Ninety percent of our day relies on faith.

Knowing that faith is part of who we are and the moments of our life that we take for granted (that the sun will come out tomorrow, that our flight will land safely), where in your business would a little more faith help out? Faith that more clients are coming? Faith that a mistake can be a good thing? Faith that you are all you need for success?

8. True faith is continued belief in the face of adversity.

Name a time in your life when faith got you through a difficult moment. It can be a time that led to a big success and a big reward. Now, what might have happened if you'd lost faith before the miracle?

How often are you doing this in your own business?

Are there times when, if you had just a little more faith, it would get you the results you were looking for?

CHAPTER 7

Being Practical

I always like to look on the optimistic side of life, but I am realistic enough to know that life is a complex matter.

—Walt Disney

Senior White House Advisor Valerie Jarrett, who also chairs the White House Council on Women and Girls, looked out across a sea of freshly graduated Wellesley women and encouraged the graduates to be resilient, but to pace themselves. "For those of you wondering if you can have it all, the answer is yes, but there is a catch," she said. "The arc of life is long, so don't expect to have it all at the same time."

There is faith, and there is practicality. There is passion and enthusiasm and there is plain old horse sense. To succeed in business, you need both. You have to be realistic about what you can accomplish and how quickly you can accomplish it. You have to be practical about the people you will need to help you do it. Finally, you have to be sensible about how isolating it can be to build a business, and how to stay connected. We have our heads down, pushing through and taking the hits as we are trying to figure it all out. And sometimes, it can make us feel incredibly alone. Isolation is both a money drain and a real downer. So you have to go out of your way to prevent it from overtaking you. When was the last time you really reached out to someone else in a big way? To a mentor, a colleague, or someone you know who "gets it"?

Your business is your *responsibility* alone; but you cannot *do it* alone. I've seen my share of big-league business owners who are trying to go at it alone, and I watch in disappointment as their companies lose steam. No matter how strong or capable we are, we *all* need help.

The more successful you become, the easier it is to become totally irrational and unpractical. You will lose sight of finding time to study, collaborate, and keep your foundation. You might even lose the ability to work. You become so distracted by people to manage and questions to answer that the simple effective work ethic you once exhibited—the very thing that got you to where you are today— goes stale.

This chapter is about being realistic in the *long term* about what it takes to make money, grow a team, or sustain a business for 50 years. I don't suggest being realistic in your visions, plans, and goals for business, but I *demand* being realistic about what it will take to get there.

As successful as you get or as many failures as you have, you must focus on the now:

- What will it take in *this moment* and at *this time* to make this plan or strategy work?
- What *systems can you put into place* that will allow you to focus and make it easier to take the next step?

These systems—even the seemingly smallest things—are what will make the biggest difference. I used to have a really cool habit; I would write three things I was going to accomplish that week on a Post-It note that I put on the front of the notebook I use daily. I didn't make a plan to accomplish them or push toward them; I just *noticed* them several times a day and knew that was the practical to-do list that would make that week successful. And I always accomplished 90 percent of them, which was pretty damn good results week after week. I just focused on *what* had to be done, not *how* it was going to actually get done.

There's so much that gets taken care of for us if we let it. When we try to fix, push, solve, and overplan, then we don't even have the space for the good stuff to enter in. Being practical allows for success to feel effortless at times. That doesn't mean you don't have to *work* for it; it just means no worry and no white knuckling.

So, ask yourself:

- What are you demanding happens right now? How is it going for you?
- What are you panicked about? How is it going for you?
- What are you doing over and over and getting the same results? How can you let it go?
- What do you *not* believe?
- What are you kidding yourself about?
- What do you *want* to believe—but don't really? Be as honest as you can.

Maybe your reach goal is:

- "I'll make a million."
- "I'll lose 30 pounds."
- "I'll buy a house."
- "I'll land a job at _____."

Believing in it and dreaming about it will get it on your to-do list. but *practical action* will make it a reality.

Practical action is what keeps you grounded regarding what has to be done. Drama is what keeps you from doing it. And that drama can actually feel good at first; it brings you attention, which can disguise itself as productivity and movement. It might even make you feel successful or accomplished in the moment. In the long haul, it doesn't help you get to your obvious solution or answers. And whether you recognize it or not, it is exhausting.

When speaking to his congregation, Reverend Michael Beckwith said most people live by the motto "I have drama, therefore I am!" Is this how you are operating in your life and business?

I know *I* do. For goodness sakes, I was a theatre major in college! If there is a raucous buzz happening, then things must be moving and shaking, right? Things *must* be getting done! What about all that drama, conflict, busy-ness, and flurry makes us feel needed or more productive?

Ever seen Busy Betty, the busiest person you've ever known? She goes and goes and goes and you can't catch up with her. Yet despite all that movement, she doesn't seem to get anything done.

Pay attention to your actions and the results of those actions, and notice what you are paying attention to. Check your energy level and your frustration level. After a while, it might become obvious that you are choosing the hard way to get a taste of the drama! Drama is simply easier for some of us to access than practical action steps. Usually, it all starts with determining your priorities.

Personal finance expert Suze Orman sometimes rings in my head when I am trying to get clear about where to go, what to do, and how to navigate the practical part of my life with the visionary side. I remember her motto, "People first, then money, then things."

It is amazing what kind of stories we create when we're trying to be perfect. Our perfectionism can skew our priorities. When you decide clearly what your priorities are, then take action on them, this confusion disappears. Remind yourself that your greatest service to yourself, your business, and your world is to *let go* of perfectionism and to stick to your priorities! That is being practical in the best way possible. You have to make certain your priorities align with your values, but you also have to make sure you remain professional.

I have to be honest; I am not even sure if we can define the parameters of professional these days. When locals from my little town in South Carolina stroll into our office, you can immediately see the look on their faces as they think to themselves, "Well they sure do things different here."

On any given day you can see dogs running from one office to the other, a gaggle of us in jeans and sunglasses, and a film crew wandering around in costumes for our next wild teaching video. I have a feeling there are lots of folks that would consider us not so professional or practical; but we are both.

I recently had Bert Jacobs, founder of the $100 million Life is Good brand, speak at one of my events. He is an amazing speaker and thought leader, but the best part was that he did the keynote in jeans, barefoot, and threw Frisbees into the crowd, all while drinking a beer.

For me, the freedom of having no corporate rules is amazing. However, I do believe there are some corporate and office principles that serve us all well and that we should revisit. After all, companies that operated according to these rules didn't become so successful without doing *something* right. There are some very practical systems in place in big business that make a lot of sense:

- Have certain *systems* in place, and *follow them.*
- Operate according to basic rules of *etiquette.*

- Keep an air of *professionalism* at all times.
- Let *facts and not emotions* drive actions.

When I see people *re*acting instead of being *pro*active—whether it's in the way they manage their time or how they react to certain business situations—it reminds me of the phenomenon of emotional business management (EBM).

Sometimes it's hard *not* to be emotional and reactive. Our business, and in fact, most businesses, are *very* personal. As entrepreneurs, we nurture them, grow them, and depend on them. We are attached, and that's understandable. But you must continue to ask yourself: What decisions and actions am I taking on emotionally as opposed to systematically? What are you doing in your business that you might never think of doing in "the office"? Get practical about this, and stop doing things that are wasting your time.

No matter how big or small, we are in business. We are as important as GE or Walmart or Wells Fargo. Somewhere along the way, small business owners have been derailed and delegated to being "soft" in business. Our contracts are fuzzy, our deals change, and our terms are meant for bending. None of this is the case. At least, it's not at *my company*. I recognize that a big key to business is to *BE business*. Have standards. Make practical decisions in hiring and firing people. Have a plan to get your money. Have a process to protect your money. This is the real path from hobbyist owner (HO) to business owner (BO).

Hobbyist owner (HO). You want to be in business. You have dreams, but no systems or plans. You have hopes, but the work ethic wanders. You have passion, but profit is less important.

Business owner (BO). You are dedicated to your vision above all else, even irrationally so. You have huge ideas and you have practical steps and support in getting there. You invest in yourself and in others. You run your business like a *business*, not like a lemonade stand.

There are times for dreaming and there are times to go to the hospital. Make time for both.

Chapter 7 Homework

1. **Faith versus practicality.**

   Are you practical about what it takes to be successful?

   Do you have a plan to turn your beliefs into reality?

   Do you understand the real difference between having a vision for your business and taking action to make it real?

   Do you understand that *hope* is not a business plan?

2. **Practical support.**

   Who do you turn to that "gets it" when it comes to your business?

   Come to think about it, do you turn to *anyone*—or do you try to go it alone?

   How's that working out for you?

3. **Your practical to-do list.**

   What three things would you like to get done this week that would make a difference in your business? List them here.

   Now, how can you keep them front and center so that you have a practical plan to get them done?

4. **Dream versus reality.** Just remember: The reason most people don't bring their dreams to life is that they're not willing to start at a time when it seems impossible in order to get to a place where they could actually happen. It's time for you to take three practical actions. After you answer the following questions, think about the next three steps.

You'll be amazed at how quickly you will make progress. Let's talk about making your dreams real.

First, list one of your big dreams that deep in your heart you would like to believe is possible, but you have some doubts about. It's okay if it's big.

Next, list three practical actions that could put you on the path toward making it a reality.

5. Drama queens (and kings).

Do you crave drama?

What drama are you taking part in that's keeping you from the practical actions that lead to success?

6. Perfectionism makes you (feel) important.

Are you trying to be perfect?

Is it keeping you from making any progress?

What might happen if you let go of perfectionism and simply focused on your priorities?

How much more could you get done?

7. HOs and BOs.

Honesty time: Are you a hobbyist owner or a business owner? List the reasons why.

If you're an HO, what practical steps can you take to earn your BO badge?

CHAPTER 8

Not Being Practical

Being realistic is the most commonly traveled road to mediocrity.

—Will Smith

Recently, a dear friend of mine was diagnosed with endometrial cancer.

We have been taught since elementary school that attitude matters. We've all heard it a million times. As adults, we understand the Buddhist principle that "thoughts become things," but it becomes much clearer when real life or death is right there in your face.

You are either choosing to live or die in every minute of every second of every day. Sadly, my friend just doesn't see things that way. Being practical helps when fighting for your life. You want to get the right answers and take the right medicine, but you always want to make sure you're taking the right path.

• • •

You likely know the announcement from television and radio: "This is a test. This is only a test. This is a test of the emergency broadcast system." I remember when I was a kid it always happened during afternoon TV—and it would scare me. Tests can be scary. I am a really poor test taker, lousy at SATs and not great during exam time.

I've been able to get rid of some of that fear over the years, and now I kind of love tests. When you work with over 300 clients at any given time, something always pops up. With tons of different energies, experiences, needs, and personalities, there is always some test being presented to you, and your rational brain tells you to be safe, be practical.

And then there are the other tests that have to do with:

- Family
- Cash flow
- Children
- Spouses
- Health
- I could go on and on.

You each have your own test. It usually appears looking like a fear, a threat, a stumble, a complaint, an unexpected event or bad news. And here is the solution: treat them just as that, a test.

The truth is that everything is a lesson waiting to be learned. There is no good. There is no bad. There is only what is. Because we have been raised to believe tests are pass or fail, we usually become overwhelmed and scared when faced with them. The fact of the matter is a test is there for us to grow, not to get it right or wrong. As the great Ben Zander said in his book *The Art of Possibility*, "Just look at it and say: FASCINATING. Then take your next step from that place."

You can't take everything that shows up in your business from a realistic or practical point of view. My friend with the cancer diagnosis saw her test as absolute. She felt she had to approach her future completely practically: "I am dying. This is hard. I'll wait and see how it plays out."

Being practical can help you live longer, but I think not being practical can save your life. It doesn't really matter what you are fighting: cancer, shyness, fear, money, wellness, love, or loss; the same applies. The monsters will always be present. How we speak to the monsters will determine our outcomes and our journey.

Change the rules.

You have some. I have some. We all do. *The money has to be made in this way. I have to do this before that. I can only invest this. I better check with this person before making that decision.*

Almost every time I have made big money, I had changed the rules, shook it up, and did things differently. I was completely unpractical because, frankly, the practical shit just wasn't working.

Take 45 seconds and list the rules you have been living by. Then take a look and consider whether they're serving you well or holding you back.

There is something magical about not being practical; it can create momentum. Remember the last time you took a vacation? Chances are you got more done the day before you left than you had the whole 30 days prior. You get stuff done when you need to, and when it counts the most.

Now, remember a time you took a wild risk; maybe you ran an ad or sent out an email and everyone responded. You can't be practical and be innovative. You can't be practical and be creative. And you can't be practical and be successful. When everyone else is zagging, you have to ZIG!

I know it will not feel logical or practical—and believe me, that's a good thing. Go in the opposite direction of everyone else to the place that no one but you can see. Use your guts and grit to say things in a different way, show up in a different place, and surprise and delight. Here's how:

Play. It will look like you are goofing off. People will ask you to hurry up, and even you will sometimes be anxious about taking the time off or being the goof. But in the end, you will get more from the play than from the practical. You will get more ideas and answers from shutting down your to-dos than you do from doing.

Question. I am sure you can find more people than you can imagine who will tell you I am annoying. I question everything. Even with a hundred pages of documented scientific facts before me, I look for the hole. I question it all. I'm not looking to prove others wrong or show that I'm right all the time. I simply wonder what both of us have left out somewhere in the middle. It's not necessarily a practical approach, but it is a really useful one.

Do things the hard way. In a world of easy access through technology, I try taking the hard way every once in a while. I show up instead of tweeting. I write a letter longhand instead of via email. I hold a live event instead of a Google hangout. The easy way frequently isn't the most profitable, and it is almost always the least creative, but sometimes it's the best way for what you're doing.

Spend. No money guru or financial planner will tell you this, but here is my dirty little secret: I've overinvested and overspent on my business many times over the years. It wasn't practical, but it worked, and I can't imagine doing it any other way. When I saw opportunities from sponsorship to hiring, I grabbed them. I'm never sure how long they will last, and I don't want to have any regrets.

Now, those were the dirty little secrets, but the way to make it work is to back it up with a practical plan. Be willing to work hard to ensure it does.

● ● ●

I almost had a heart attack about three years ago when I read Suze Orman's new book *The Money Class: How to Stand in Your Truth and Create the Future You Deserve*. When I got to the chapter on business, I saw a checklist, essentially a list of items that signal that it's time to shut down your company. I was so taken aback when I saw it because over the last three years, I had experienced everything on the checklist more than once.

If I followed that advice, I would have been out of business. Which just goes to show that while the path I took might not have been practical, it kept me in the game. Being totally impractical works.

Confused yet? You should be, since I told you last chapter to get your practical ass in line! It's like all things that work well: It requires balance. You must have both ends of the spectrum functioning—and you can bet you are out of balance when your business feels stale or stagnant. You can bet you have traded one for the other to feel more security, and it's time to start tipping the scale in the other direction.

Chapter 8 Homework

1. **Your rule book.**

   Got rules? Good. Let's list them out. C'mon, you know you have them. They are the rules you know you live by.

   If you were brave enough to list them, now let's discuss if they're helping you or holding you back.

2. **Be practically impractical.**

   Have you been impractical in your path towards success? Have you ever broken the rules or taken action that others told you not to?

   Where are you being so practical in your own life that it is actually to your own detriment?

3. **Rules others live by.**

   Name the rules other people you know seem to live by. Do you unconsciously follow them?

   What might happen if you stopped listening and did the opposite?

4. **Taking bad advice.**

   Are you heeding bad advice?

   Do you let anyone and everyone influence you, or do you only listen to a group of selected few?

   What might happen if you became more discerning in who you actually listened to?

CHAPTER 9

Money

"Lack of money is the root of all evil."

—Mark Twain

You know the saying about money being the root of all evil, but actually, the opposite is true. The lack of money is the root of all evil. I am no stock market expert, and I certainly do not claim to be, but this I know for sure: To make or to lose money in the market, you have to first invest in the market. Like the saying goes, "You have to be in it to win it."

So take a moment and think about this. Seriously, grab a pen and paper: How much do you spend on your car every year? (Include payments, insurance, tune-ups, gas, etc.) Ok, got that number? Take a long look at it. If you are spending a similar amount or *less* on your business, take a pause.

How do we expect to have a thriving company that helps people if you spend more on your car than on your business? It's crazy! I remember the first time I figured this out; it was a real eye opener. I quickly realized that if I do not treat my business coaching, programs, workshops, and seminars as investments in me, my future, and those I want to serve, then my business would never grow.

The first year I applied this idea of making investments in myself via coaching, programs, and building a team—my income doubled. And the best part: The number of people I was serving more than quadrupled.

When we invest in ourselves, we build a portfolio for success.

Many people have asked me how to determine the *best* investment for their business. I can't provide a cut-and-dried answer because every company has so many variables at play, but there are some things that consistently deliver benefits:

- Marketing programs and consulting where you get a specific plan.
- Opportunities where you will be in front of your ideal clients.
- The right team members to grow the business in the right areas.
- Programs where you receive mentoring from people who are where you want to be.
- Workshops and events that keep you connected and motivated.

- Software and programs that allow you to systematize and streamline.

What and how you invest will be different for each person; but investing in the first place is the key. A car cannot run without gas, a stock cannot rise without being purchased, and a business cannot run without investment fuel.

You must be ready and willing, financially, to invest money in your business. Sometimes this means being certain you have a cash flow through other means until your business is soaring. You may want to build *while* you are in a job, which is what I did. You may want to have a part-time job to create savings to use for a year. Whatever you decide to do, it is critical to have a financial plan to invest in your business portfolio.

Our economy and stock market are all over the place these days; therefore, the only *sure* investment is the one you make in *you*. It might be easier to know what *your* return will be. If you rely on what your experiences have taught you, your business can grow—regardless of what the stock market does. Investing in yourself is a definite way to grow financially and personally.

I can't grow enough. I keep trying, but I can't. I'm always looking for the next thing I need. I ask you to do the same. Keep chasing the dream and investing in yourself! I remember the first time I spent almost $15,000 on my business. Did I gulp? Yep. Did I have five minutes of buyer's remorse? Yep. But then I said to myself, "Every dollar I invest in myself comes back three-, four-, fivefold in income, understanding, success, and sustainability."

Because I live on the water, I spend a lot of time observing the tides. I love them, and the message they send: that every day, something has to leave to later return. Investing is like the tides. Just like the water needs to keep moving, so does your money, and I have found that the moment you invest in your business, it always has a boom.

Is it magical thinking? No. I just keep investing in myself and know that it is always a better investment than anything else. Business is expensive, and not just in terms of financial cost. It takes time, commitment, and effort. Do you know a business owner who won't go to the networking event because they have to pay for parking or breakfast or travel? You do. You may have even been one.

There is no convenient time or place to become successful. I built my business with this understanding. I did it by *going to the yes*, because it does not come to you, knock on the door, and deliver a payday. As Thomas Edison said, "Opportunity is missed by most people because it's dressed in overalls, and looks like work."

So here's the big idea; I am going to lay it out fast and dirty. If you can get these rules about money right, you can make millions. Here are all the places not to be cheap, so you don't attract cheap:

1. **Don't get cheap help.** Do I really have to say anything else? It seems obvious. It's natural to want to save money here and there, but you get what you pay for. Ever think, "If this coach/consultant is so good, why do they charge so little?" You should. I know I do.
2. **Don't get cheap business cards.** I always forget to bring my business cards. (I know!) If you are going to have them, have them say, "I'm valuable!"
3. **Don't go networking or speaking in cheap clothes.** I cannot tell you how many smart, savvy, fun people I've met who look as if they have put absolutely no effort into showing up as their best self. It's distracting! I don't pretend to be a fashionista; but I want and make every attempt to look my best, feel my best, and show up as my best self.
4. **Don't be cheap with your resources.** Give away your best and they will buy the rest. I hate when people tease you in an attempt to make more money. If you stand by your services, are great at what you do, and love people up, they will want more.
5. **Don't be cheap with your time.** Business takes effort. When I hear people say they don't want to work hard, I am clear on their best path: to get a job working for someone else. Business takes hustle; if you love what you do, it won't feel like work. If you're cheap with your time, your results will reflect that.

6. **Find a rich mentor.** Deliver rich resources and results. If you invest richly in your business, you will reap rich rewards!

● ● ●

Money commands respect. Money deserves attention. Money responds to love. I love to talk about money. I particularly love to talk about the impact money can have on people, the planet, and its ability to foster change. Most of you are reading this because you want to make more money and you want to make a difference. Making a difference starts with your behavior—but it launches from how you respect money.

Money is energy. The greater respect you have for it, the more vibrantly that energy returns to you.

The rules for prosperity are simple:

1. **Honor commitments.** When you agree to pay for a service, product, program, or item, follow through. Pay your bills on time if you expect others to pay you.
2. **Take 100 percent responsibility.** When shit happens (and it will), take 100 percent responsibility for your finances and communicate with people. People that show up and are willing will always work problems out.
3. **Treat your business like a business.** Ally Financial, Ford Motor Credit, and Capital One do not let people dishonor their obligations, so why would you? We certainly do not have to behave like Big Brother, but we could learn a few things from larger corporations about having policies and procedures regarding payments in our business.
4. **Hold the space.** My business requires people to meet their obligations and commitments. We always work with willing and responsive people; but in the cases that we don't, we have legal standard operating procedures. In other words, we treat our business like a real business—because it is.

5. **Pass your money on.** Everyone talks about charitable giving; I'm talking about non-charitable. How much do you tip? Do you spread the wealth? Do you know that giving brings you more (even though it does *not* get you a tax break)?

6. **Love your money.** Watch it. Keep an eye on it. Make sure it has a house that takes care of it and brings more of it to you. Track and protect your money.

7. **Don't play dumb.** Money likes and is attracted to smart people. It likes you to know where it is, how it behaves, and where it goes. The fastest way to go broke is to not know how your money is performing.

8. **Do the hard stuff.** Talk to clients and customers about their bills, what they owe, and give them the truth about money. When you shy away from money issues with your clients, you shy away from abundance. Money is not the most important thing in the world, but it touches everything that is. If you aren't paying your bills or holding the space for your clients to pay theirs, you are out of money alignment.

Remember: Money commands respect. Money deserves attention. Money responds to love. And money doesn't want you to *"wait until the time is right."*

People often tell me that they're waiting to start their business or one of my programs or to make a change until when the time is right—or when they have the money to do it. Without being disrespectful, that kind of response is laughable to me for a few reasons: First, it's ridiculous to believe that we are actually in that much control—and that money will somehow magically fall into our laps if we wait long enough and keep doing what we've been doing. Second, it means you believe that anything more than just a delay in your destiny is out of integrity. And third, if you have thought of it, even for a nanosecond, then the time is now.

There is no way to ever find enough money to launch. Even the big software guys that launch with millions would prefer to wait and have even more millions. Accurate thinking will tell you that life is just a series of moments, and the more you wait, the more you wait.

It seems simple because it is.

I don't think there is a right time for someone to die any more than there is a right time for someone to be born. I don't believe in meditating on or pondering the right time to launch a business or get the help you need. You feel it, and then you do it. You might think that kind of approach, failing to think about something carefully enough, can get you in trouble. But I will tell you the trouble it has gotten me in is the best kind. I was moving forward. Maybe I looked a little foolish or wasn't quite ready, but so what? The payoff was worth it. The reward was no more waiting.

I know some of you are scared, and that's why it doesn't seem like the right time. I feel you. I really, *really* do. Fear is the biggest factor in waiting. Fear will always make you wonder.

I recently sent an email to my list of subscribers that essentially said, "Get off your ass!" A lot of people wanted to opt out. I wonder why that struck them so deeply. Have you been sitting on your rear a bit too long? If you want to change the world, are you willing to first change *your* world?

Are you willing to work extra, save more, spend less, and get this business off the ground? There is only one *right time*—and you are living in it as you read this. Money will come, but I have never seen all of it show up before you launch or grow your business. Don't wait on the money to make more money.

● ● ●

Now for the fun part.

What do you do once you make the money? Pay yourself first. Let me repeat. Pay yourself first. Right after taxes is you. After you comes all the rest.

Too many business owners—especially women—forget, don't plan, or don't budget to pay themselves. Many don't even budget at all. Visa's International Barometer of Women's Financial Literacy survey was conducted with 25,000 male and female participants in 27 countries. American women ranked among the top five in only one category: budgeting. While 53.4 percent said they follow a budget, 24.2 percent said they don't even have one—or they don't have enough money for a budget.

Not budgeting is a really great way to lose sight of your business growth and shortcomings. Not budgeting to pay yourself is a path to burnout. We can love what we do, be passionate and enthusiastic all day long, but if we end up taking nothing for ourselves, then we will burn ourselves out. That's when the work becomes much more like work.

Always remember that, by definition, business is the practice of making one's living by engaging in commerce. You have to make money to be in business and you have to take the first crop of that business for yourself, or the family starves.

My dad was the sixth generation of Jonathans to farm the same area of land. When you are the seventh generation of a farming family, you learn a few things about how things grow, and growing corn isn't all that different from growing a business:

1. **Pay attention.** Too much water is deadly. Too little water is deadly. You have to find the middle ground.
2. **Take the first harvest for yourself.** Put some corn on the family table, and you will eat all summer. Then, sell the rest.
3. **Plant a variety.** Tomatoes take three months to grow. You can eat them early. Avocados take three years, but yields a higher price. Take care of the today and then focus on the higher profit tomorrow.

Here is the full process in a nutshell:

- Don't wait to have money to go make some.
- Invest some to make more.
- Give your money time and attention.
- Keep what you make.

- You take first.
- Have a plan to make more for a higher-yield long term.
- Give money in generosity.

Rinse. Repeat. Then rinse again.

Chapter 9 Homework

1. **Spending habits.** I asked you to calculate how much you spent on your car versus your business. Are you *seriously* not investing in your business?

   Did that make you feel dumb, bad, or guilty? Good. Because now I hope you see how important it is.

2. **The best investments.**

   Based on where your business is, list the top three investments you need to make and why. Get honest.

   What will help you grow faster, quicker?

   Where have you been cheap in an attempt to save money, even if it is costing you in the long run?

3. **You get what you pay for, right?**

   Where are you being cheap in your business? C'mon, you know where you are. Let's just get this out of the way and start being honest.

4. **Money commands respect.**

   Do you respect your money?

   Do you respect others?

   Do you honor your commitments regarding money?

   Do you pay on time?

   Do you know that the way you treat money is a direct reflection of how you treat clients and opportunities? It's true.

5. **Waiting for the right time.**

   Are you waiting for the perfect moment? So often, we wait for the money to come first before we take action.
   What are you waiting for?
   What are you waiting to invest in?

6. **Budgeting.** Some important questions around your budget:

   Do you have one?
   Do you pay yourself first?
   Do you know where your money goes? If not, it's time to figure that out.

7. **Your business is your livelihood.** Always remember that, by definition, business is the practice of making one's living by engaging in commerce.

   There's no question here. I just wanted to reinforce the importance of this definition.

8. **Tomatoes and avocados.**

   Are you planting solely short-term yields (tomatoes) or planning for the long term (avocados)?
   List which investments are which, and why you are making them part of your business.

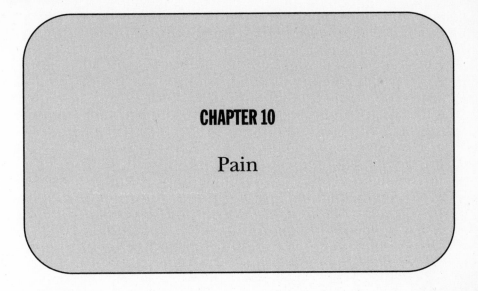

CHAPTER 10

Pain

It's so hard to forget pain, but it's even harder to remember sweetness.
We have no scar to show for happiness. We learn so little from peace.
—Chuck Palahniuk, *Diary*

Turn off CNN, put down the *Wall Street Journal*, and ask your friends to be silent for just a few days. If you stop leaning on the pain you hear, see, and feel, interesting things can happen.

If you just look around, you'll see so much abundance right now. Look at your children, your pets, your health, your friends, and your stuff that you love: the car or house or fun hobby. Look at the pictures in your house of vacations traveled, holidays, and events. The sense of abundance is overflowing. It is truly plentiful.

Stop living based on what's going on Wall Street, or you will always be disappointed. Start living in the economy of now, and the economy of plenty. This outlook will alter every thought you have and decision you make.

Pain does crazy things. It enables us to make poor decisions, compels us to say *no*, stopping us from taking action—letting fear dictate our choices.

What pain in your life are you leaning on? None of us are going to escape pain. We signed up for it when we were born. But there are two types of pain: that which paralyzes, and that which allows us to perform. On the one hand, pain paralysis is that wound, that mess, that debilitating feeling of defeat that can last for a day, a week, sometimes even a year. Pain paralysis stops you from doing anything. Pain that drives performance, on the other hand, is when you take your wound or mess and use it as motivation for business good. Make your mess channel your message.

I teach my clients to do this by emphasizing the power of telling their own stories as they start their own businesses. We start with the phrase: Your truth will set you free.

One of the biggest neon-light mistakes that I see professionals make is believing that their pain has nothing to do with business. They say, "I need to focus on the clients and what the clients need. I need to make sure that I'm working toward solving their problems, and paying attention to their struggles."

They forget to tell their own stories.

There's nothing that I hate more than reading a canned bio on someone's website or in their marketing materials. I know, you're probably protesting, "But I'm *supposed* to have a bio on my website. I'm supposed to have an 'About Me' on my website." Bios are credentials and for the most part are pretty boring. The fascinating stuff—the stuff that enables you to connect with someone, really care about someone, and develop a sense of empathy—comes when you know their story. This is so vitally important when you are building relationships with potential clients.

Don't tell the Cinderella version of your story. Tell the ugly stepsister, warped version. Your trials and tribulations are the best thing you can use to encourage your clients to find their own success.

I'll share something I did when beginning my business. Had I known what I know now, I certainly would have done it differently: I worked way too hard in the beginning. Way too hard! I put in a lot of unnecessary hours. I will admit to that. I also took on every client that came my way. If I could nab them, I took them. That didn't serve me well in the long run.

I also followed the word of marketing "gurus." I believed that if I did everything their way, it would work for me; that, as they had promised, their success would be my success. The only result was that I was exhausted, a little bit confused, and really frustrated. I ended up not having a core message.

I thought, "I've got to have a name. It's got to be cute. It's got to appeal to people. It's got to be as big as Pepsi and Coca-Cola." That only made me exhausted. It came to the point where I stopped trying to create this fantasy business. So screw it. I decided to say, "This is who I am. The best thing that I have to offer is me."

And so I did.

Your truth will set them free.

Your journey, your mistakes, the way you overcame obstacles and your conclusions—that is the insight your clients are looking for.

You know that your bio should include everything that you've accomplished. Maybe you talk about where you went to school or your 67 credentials. Maybe you want to mention your kids or your family. Those things are important as well. People like to hear about them. But what's most important is more than that: Why you? What's your story? Why should your clients care about it? What has it taught you that you can pass along to them?

Let's say you're going to work with parents who have difficulties with their kids. You're going to be a parenting coach. Why are you coming to this area? What advice and experience do you have to bring to other parents? Did you struggle as a parent initially, then make a real turnaround? Something you want to share with other people? Was it that you had an extraordinary parenting situation that maybe wasn't so pleasant but taught you a lot that other people can learn from?

If you're a health coach, what's your story around health? You wouldn't be drawn to something that you don't have a story about. You wouldn't care enough to make a career out of it if you didn't have a stake in it—something in your life brought you to it.

People need to connect to your story. They need to see and connect with your struggle. Don't shy away from everything about yourself, both the impressive and the not-so-impressive. Be authentically you and people will love you for it.

If you answer, "Oh, I don't know what my story is. I have no pain. No one wants to hear about my mess." Then I ask you to really dig deep, because I promise you it's there. It may be covered up; it may be something that you're afraid to share, but it's definitely there. So share it. It is what opens people up and makes them *want* to do business with you. Pain is powerful for profits.

● ● ●

Will Smith gave an acceptance speech during Nickelodeon Kids' Choice Awards one year where he encouraged kids to focus on two activities: running and reading: "There is no problem or pain that has not already happened to someone and they have written about it. And if you can outsmart that head in your voice when you are running that says stop, quit, or you are too tired, you can outlast anything."

I love when I see the power of pushing through, learning, and doing whatever it takes. It is the key ingredient for business success. If your outlook is that it's okay to give up because of the pain—or think you are too old, too lazy, too confused or too insignificant—then you might want to get a desk job. Believe me, it will be easier—a lot easier. But what if you believed you were:

- Never too small?
- Never too old?
- Never too scared?
- Never too behind?
- Never too broken?
- Never too tired?

Let the following two stories inspire you to work harder, smarter, and faster today. They are stories about my father and my nanny.

My dad is 72 years old, and has never used a computer. He dropped out of college at 21 to come back home and run the family farm after his father died. He is a seventh-generation farmer on the same land that has been in his family for years. He has spent more time on a combine than anywhere else in his life.

I decided to get him an iPhone. I was nervous. He was too. I could tell he was scared. He had just gotten used to a cell phone, and here I was forcing this fancy new kind on him. But he was game—like always.

I got my risky nature from my dad. After just a few hours learning the ropes of his new device, he was texting. It does take him a long while to type, but he's doing it! And when I got him on Safari, the browser, I said, "Dad, you can type anything in the world you would want to read or learn about here. What do you most want to see?" He typed in "John Deere." When the site came up, he beamed.

I had never seen someone get on the Internet for the first time. I was so proud of him because I knew he was scared and did it anyway. Never be too scared to try something new.

When I was growing up, I had a nanny named Lilly Mae. She came from a long line of Southern farm hands. She had no formal education, but she was incredibly hardworking. She raised lots of babies and wiped a lot of butts by the time she was 78 years. Just a week ago, she came into my dad's hardware store and said, "Mr. Evans, I am exhausted."

My dad asked her if she was okay. She told him she had gone back to school to get a degree in early childhood development. At 78 years old, she decided it was time to formalize what she had been doing all those years. Whatever you think you're too old for, you are *never* too old.

Business and life are both tests. None of us are "born into" greatness or success; we earn those things. We go through the pain to get the reward. The line in the sand is always how far you are willing to go, how brave you are willing to be, and whether you can take the pain and keep going.

The systems and desk work, that's the easy part. You can set that up with software; but a system or software cannot make you brave. You have to do that work. You have to use that pain. The painful place where 90 percent of entrepreneurs are not willing to go is the exact place where people make a lasting business. That alone will put you ahead of the pack.

Most people would choose being comfortable over being uncomfortable. We are conditioned to run from pain and shy away from hurt. After all, we are a nation full of people who get a certificate for participating. Participating is your duty. Everyone is obligated to show up, but going beyond participation while ignoring the pain is where the reward lies.

I learned my greatest lessons about pain from my mama. Anyone who has met her is transformed—not sure for better or for worse, but most definitely transformed!

Every bit of piss and vinegar I have in me came from her. She is to the point, a little in your face, but sensitive and soft underneath it all. She was a basketball coach and lives by the motto "Unless it's bleeding, keep playing."

I'll admit, I could have used a bit more nurturing at times growing up. But something she has always said to me, even to this day, has shaped me into who I am. It's five simple words: "It'll be fine; keep going." It was her response to sore throats, broken hearts, lost money, sprained ankles, missed opportunities, big wins, fear, frustration, you name it. And it really works for most situations.

And so after 39 years of hearing that "It'll be fine; keep going," I think it is finally sinking in. No matter how bad the pain is, it will be fine if you keep going. When life seems overwhelming, hard, scary, or painful, it will all be fine; keep going.

We all look to what others are doing, how they are doing it, and what seems normal. You have to be willing to do a 180 when needed, a complete turnaround from your current position. We tend to slide in at 20 degrees or 50 degrees because 180 is too uncomfortable and too painful.

When I take the "Band-Aid" approach, the results just come faster. You know what I mean: You can slowly remove the Band-Aid or you can rip it off fast. A little pain, but it's quick and it's over. Stop leaning in and leap.

Think of what is not working in your business, marketing, life, or career: Don't try to fix it or change it; just 180 degree it. Make a complete and total change from the way it currently is. So, what is the 180 for you?

Look at it this way: You would turn around if you were driving in the wrong direction. If your relationship, job, or business is going in the wrong direction, you also have to turn around, despite the pain. You don't have to keep going in the wrong direction just to convince yourself you're right.

I know the struggles that come with that; I had a need to be right for a long time. And for about 30 years, it kept me in a job I hated. My max earning was about $50k, I had no free time, and I had created a situation where I could hardly make any of my own decisions. It became clear to me that being right was no longer serving me. In fact, it was flat-out painful. I went as far as actually believing that I wasn't really interested in seeking therapy or coaching—at all, period. I realized I was deeply afraid they might make me wrong. I told myself that it would be painful, and I would rather just be comfortable in the shit I had currently created.

Some people will get tired of living like that. They will realize that they're holding onto assumptions, ideas, and the need to be right—and that it won't get them to their desired life. The pain of being sick and tired eventually becomes worse than the pain of staying the same.

Honestly, the number-one reason I see entrepreneurs struggle, suffer, and often quit is because they can't let go of the need to be right. You cannot have a new life, more business, or growth without the willingness to stretch and be called out on the BS.

So, do you want be right, or do you want be rich?

You can't hold onto both desires. Growing a business, changing your life, getting clients, and making money requires admitting that you are wrong. It takes sacrifice. And sacrifice means doing something you have never done to get something you have never had.

It takes pain. You can't sacrifice *and* hold onto to being right.

Below is a list I've compiled of the things people most frequently do and say that sabotages their success. Make sure you clean this list up and move into openness, willingness, and readiness to *change* (even when painful):

1. **"Yes, but."** "Yes, but" will keep you stuck in your excuses around time, money, and knowledge. Just remove this phrase from your vocabulary. I have my private clients take improv class, because the number-one rule of improv is *yes*! Start changing the "yes, but" to "yes, and."

   Reframe: Anything worth doing is worth doing poorly to start with!

2. **"I quit."** This is always the easiest—and what we perceive to be the least painful—answer. It can be a quick solution, after all. But guess what? Nothing changes when we quit.

Reframe: I get exactly what I need when I need it. Is quitting going to move me closer to my dreams?

3. **"I didn't get what I needed."** Blame is evil. I know; I did it for years. It makes us feel better about something when it isn't out fault. It also doesn't move us forward or change our outcomes.

   Reframe: I am 100 percent responsible for everything that happens to me—good, bad, or in between.

4. **"There isn't enough [time, money, resources, help]."** When we are working from a lack of anything, we simply get more of the same.

   Reframe: Everything I need is already present. And there is more than enough.

5. **"That hurt my feelings."** Feelings are choices. When we choose hurt or negativity, we then send that energy out in a ripple effect through the world.

   Reframe: I choose how I feel about everything. No one can make me feel anything. That is my choice. If I am offended, the offense is within me.

6. **"I'm not listening."** Even people who are working with coaches or in programs are not always willing to really do what is required, or fully listen to outside guidance.

   Reframe: I have chosen this person or this path for a reason, and I am willing to do what is required even if I don't understand how right now—and even if it might make me wrong.

When we step up to responsibility in all we do, we have to step into some discomfort. It's simply the nature of growth. We have to experience pain and eliminate the need to be right and the fear of sacrifice. To truly help more people, you have to be willing to help yourself. To be the change in the world, you have to change. Change is pain, and it starts with being okay with letting go. If we can let go of being right and not care who gets the credit for what, then we can change the world over and over and over again.

Finally, find someone that recognizes pain and can support you through it.

As an entrepreneur, life is going to come in tsunamis if you are risking, working, and sacrificing. Sometimes the basket of BS we are holding is just too damn big to carry ourselves. This is a message I share with my clients when I know the pain level is on turbo-charge. If that's about how you feel right now—uncomfortable, in pain, and scared—I share it with you, too.

I love you.

I love you when you're wrong.

I love you when I'm wrong.

I love you when you succeed.

I love you when you hiccup.

I love you when you celebrate.

I love you when you procrastinate.

My private motto has always been: "If I love them, I can coach them. If I always love them, I can hold the space for the hard stuff." Never forget, this too shall pass. Pain is just the business getting stronger while you do the next hard thing. *"It'll be fine; keep going."*

Chapter 10 Homework

1. Pain is part of the game.

How do you deal with pain?

Does it lead to paralysis or performance?

Name a time when you took action despite the pain. What were your results? Now think of a time when the pain stopped you. What might have happened had you kept going?

(continued)

(*continued*)

Which results do you prefer?

What can you learn from this?

2. **Make your mess your message.**

Are you sharing your pain? Do you neglect to share your stories at the expense of your clients having a better understanding of you?

List 2 "pain stories" that taught you about life.

How powerful would it be if you shared this with your present and potential clients?

3. **Cinderella versus the ugly stepsister.**

Have you been telling the polished version of your story?

What would happen if you let people see the warts?

Think about who you might connect with. Is it the "perfect" folks or the ones with a little bit of tarnish on them?

4. **What are you "too..."?** Too scared? Too old? Too inexperienced? Too broke?

What if you just dropped the story and realized that anything you think you're "too..." to do is just a state of mind?

5. **Certificate of participation.**

Are you trying to get credit for just showing up?

What would happen if you didn't need accolades and you went beyond just participating?

6. **180 it.**

What's not working today?

What if you did a 180, ripped off the Band-Aid, and just made a difference right now?

What would happen if you simply stepped *into* the pain?

7. **Being right.**

Do you have this need? Where and when do you need to be right?

How's it helping you? How's it hurting you?

Truth time: Would you rather be right or rich?

8. **100 percent responsible.**

Are you blaming others for the things that aren't working in your life?

List all the things you think are wrong due to outside forces. Now ask yourself if you'd be willing to take 100 percent responsibility for them. Does that make you feel empowered or less in control?

How does that affect how you would attack those problems?

9. **The painful truth.**

Answer honestly: Is it okay to quit despite the pain? Answer yes or no.

If you choose yes, great. It's probably time to get a job. No judgment; just honesty. I'm just telling you if you feel that way, you can make your life a hell of a lot easier if you just get a job.

If you choose no, good for you. Keep reading. The pain will subside.

CHAPTER 11

Time

We must use time wisely and forever realize that the time is always ripe to do right.

—Nelson Mandela

To be more successful in our lives and more efficient in our relationships, business, and the world, we must first get clear about our vision for where we are going. To help do that:

- Your decisions should be intuitive and quick.
- Clarity should be part of a daily meditative practice.
- You should play with your vision daily.
- You should create a weekly list of what you need and want.
- You should *ask* for what you need within 30 minutes of needing it.

This brings us to the topic of time. Let's begin with two important questions:

- How are you *wasting time* in your life and business?
- How are *others* wasting your time?

Whatever time is being wasted, I implore you to end it—right now. I have a clear refund policy when I do one-on-one work with clients: I can't get my time back, so you can't get your money back. And time is *far* more valuable than money.

I don't just teach about marketing, business, and building; I practice what I preach. I know it works in such a way that I can get more done in an hour than most people can complete in a week. It starts with not turning excuses into reasons. That burns through time like you have never seen.

How much time have you spent waiting on a yes?

Waiting on a deal?

Waiting on a client?

Waiting on an answer?

You can wait on a *no*, but if you need a *yes*, you gotta *go to it*! No *yeses* ever come to you. You have to grab them.

One of the earliest challenges I faced when building my business was the size of my database. I had an extremely responsive list and a great relationship with them, but it was small. I wasted months trying to decide how to grow that list fast.

I knew a woman who I wanted to help me do it. I wanted her to participate in an online event that would bring prospects to my database list. I felt her audience was right for me, and she had over 25,000 people who had signed up to be part of her mailing list.

However, she didn't return my emails. Her assistant turned everything down from me, and she was hard to get to. Trying to connect to her was taking forever, and I didn't have that kind of time. There were only two pieces of information at my disposal:

1. She was on Twitter, so I casually connected with her there.
2. She was going to be attending a seminar in Florida that was a few weeks out.

This would be an interesting time-saving solution. But there was a problem: I was broke and working a day job. But that excuse wasn't enough for me, so I booked a ticket immediately.

I flew down, met this woman and explained to her *why* she should help me, how we could work together, and that it would be very difficult for her to turn down such an action-taker *in person*. (I didn't mention I used the last space left on my credit card to buy the ticket. I didn't want to overwhelm her.)

She said yes, and her assistant emailed me confirmation. Meanwhile, four people at the conference told me that they had been trying to get her on a call for over a year. The moral is this: *You* have to *go* to the *yes*. Waiting on answers is a time killer—and time is money.

So, what's stopping you? You can turn every excuse you have into a reason and you will still have a *no*. Waiting, distractions, and indecision are the trifecta of lost time.

A few weeks ago I was multitasking while grilling some burgers and I burned the heck out of my finger. You know that moment when you want to scream and kick something because it hurts so badly? Well, I was sitting there thinking of all the reasons why this happened, it dawned on me *why* I had burned myself. I was *distracted*. I was focused on something *other than my goal*.

This happens constantly in our businesses. We *burn* ourselves over and over by allowing distractions to rule us. Then we ask why we can't catch a break or why nothing seems to be working.

So, what is the *big* distraction for you? How can you eliminate or change it immediately? Chances are that whatever is distracting you is always what's wasting time in your business, and that time waster is your money leak.

So what's your distraction?

Is it a worry? Money, time, resources? Is it a friend or family member who doesn't believe in your dream?

Is it making typos? (I always giggle when people tell me I have typos. I don't care. How is that a distraction from my purpose?)

Is it another business or job? Trying to do too much!?

Is it an old story that keeps replaying itself?

Is it your environment?

If you can eliminate or change the distraction, then you can uncover your solution.

The wealth-conscious entrepreneur understands that values, standards, and efficiency not only serve your business model; they serve your clients and customers. Is your business running organically, and a little on the fly? Do you waste time with each new action you take because you reinvent it every time? Do you have policies, guidelines, and procedures in place?

Here are five *must-haves* to make sure your business runs on time.

1. **Honor your commitments.** In business, as in life, your commitment is your word. Be on time, be ready, and overdeliver. We all make mistakes; but you need to show up and follow

through. If you have a product going out, be certain it goes out on time. If you are delivering a service, make certain you deliver it as promised. You may assume that these are obvious things; but stop and think:

- Am I honoring every commitment at the absolute highest level?
- Whose time might I be wasting—including my own?

2. **Set an example.** I read a great anonymous quote the other day: "Your sermon is best told by your life and not your lips." Make certain you are a model for your business and services. Your appearance, presence, energy, and language all represent you and everything you offer.

   It is easy to get busy in the day to day and forget what we are sharing with people. Sometimes it can be the smallest thing that someone picks up on, and that is the image they carry forever. Preach through your actions and your words. Distraction is the enemy. Your brand and your message is everywhere you are. Take the time to be on point.

3. **Run your business like a business.** Best practices apply no matter what stage you're in. You do not avoid policies, efficiencies, and procedures because your business is small or just starting out. To truly help and support, you run your business clean and clear.

   Establish policies, have them in writing, and make sure your team and clients understand them. Keep all conversations and communication on a business level and remind yourself why you are running this company. Make sure your business is serving everyone's highest interest by being clear and well informed.

4. **Have a mentor.** You can save a ton of time when you have a seasoned person to go to for guidance and support. Someone who has already failed, flipped, or flopped at what you are doing can help you, because you can learn from their mistakes *and* their successes. As one of my mentors always says, "Business is messy." It can be infinitely valuable to have someone to use

114

as a sounding board, to ask and gain advice from—so you can leverage your best interests in business growth.

5. **Be flexible.** Change is good. It's not always easy and not always comfortable; but it means something is shifting.

Being uncomfortable in your business and stretching yourself beyond the comfort zone means you are *not* in hobby mode. You can begin to worry if everything is perfect and you are carefree. It is in the discomfort and the required flexibility to deal with it that we find better solutions and more profitable directions.

6. **Follow up.** Money, business, and service is in the follow-up! Not just one time; but multiple, repeated follow-ups.

Save yourself the time of waiting and *be ready* in follow-up mode. Getting a no is as powerful as getting a yes. When we have an answer, we gain time. Whether it's a yes or a no, you are able to move on.

Be bold in your follow-up by asking specifically for what you want. This is where most people fail and lose time. If you have an immediate and strong call to action that saves you and the customer valuable time, you'll be ahead of game.

Here's an example: When I am filling a group or new program, I make the following touches *after* the program:

- Send the recording of my offer if it's an online program.
- Offer a private session for discussion.
- Offer a last chance for that session.
- Offer a last chance to sign up for the program.
- Personally email/contact people who were interested.
- Ask the people who've declined what they might need that is not this program.

Before an event, we touch our database 10 to 20 times.

A colleague of mine has told me that he has 100 touches planned for his next event. Follow-up and touches are where the money is and where the time saving is.

● ● ●

Here is a normal day for me:

I contacted over 20 people to work with me, wrote a portion of my book, coached five to seven clients, and had management meetings with the executive team.

There is no finish line. Grab every opportunity. Hustle. That's how it works. Like everyone who gets a lot done, I do have a few productivity tricks; but the real secret is hustle. I have learned (the hard way) that I can only do one thing at a time. So my motto regarding time is: "Get that one damn thing done as soon as possible. Then hustle to the next best thing."

Recently, I felt a little unmotivated at a very unfortunate time. It could have been spring fever or the upcoming season finale of *Nashville*, but I was stuck and there was quite a bit I needed to accomplish. I procrastinated for a while until I reminded myself of something:

Why do you have to do *everything*?

Why not do just a *little* something? Choose one small task, and go from there.

I firmly believe that action breeds action, and when I first started my business, this is what I lived by: Do one thing a day. It can be huge or it can be tiny, but do one thing.

I revisited that and committed to doing one small thing. And wouldn't you know, it snowballed. I got a lesson done, wrote a marketing plan for a new business for which I am doing marketing consulting, updated a talk, and rewrote some copy.

We can often get obsessed with *all* we have to do in our life and in our business. How about today you do just a little and see where that takes you?

I am reminded daily that if this were easy, everyone would do it. The lists and the to-dos are a long and winding road:

- The phone calls.
- The late night emails.
- The team member who quits.
- The new-hire interviews.

- The missed opportunities.
- The travel.
- The hours.
- The risk.

So why do we do it? Everyone reading this is super smart, willing, and hardworking. You could be employed and keep things simple. So why go beyond that? Because:

- We have something to say.
- We need a lot of space to say it.
- We are a little nuts.
- We are dreamers.
- We are the ones that keep the employees' dreams alive.
- We are the ones who care so much we take the hard road.
- We have something to change.

And we typically don't care how much time it takes until it starts costing us money.

For those of you pulling a late night or an early morning, for those finishing copy or texting a client, for those of you delivering more than you promised, for those of you digging deep to give back more, for those of you risking it all, for those of you innovating, for those of your doing it despite the fear…

Do it with hustle.

Chapter 11 Homework

1. Go to the yes.

Do you wait for the yes, or do you actively seek it?

If you're waiting, what is it specifically you are waiting for?

What if you just went out and grabbed it?

(continued)

(continued)

2. **Disastrous distractions.**

   What's distracting you?

   What if you just eliminated it, changed it, or delegated it?

   What might happen if you stopped being distracted and got done what needed to get done?

3. **Running your business like a business.**

   Do you have policies and procedures in place to support you?

   If not, list the ways it's likely hurting your time and productivity.

   Now, guess what? It's probably even worse than that.

4. **How's your follow-up?**

   How many times do your ask for the sale?

   Do you give up before the yes?

   Do you get upset about the no?

   Do you know that it's better to get a no than a maybe? Better to let them make a decision and move on.

5. **Multitasking is evil.**

   Do you try to do multiple things at once, believing it will save you time?

   Does it?

   Would you be better served focusing on one task at a time, with a focused approach? How might that actually save you time?

CHAPTER 12

Competition

There are two kinds of people, those who do the work and those who take the credit. Try to be in the first group; there is less competition there.

—Indira Gandhi

When you think of that person, you can't help but grimace.

It seems as though everything they do works better, looks nicer, and flows easier.

You say to yourself:

"I wish I had her life."

"He has it easy because…"

"She doesn't understand."

"He drives me nuts."

"She gets everything she wants."

"He is going to be a nightmare."

"She and I will never get along."

We have all felt that way about someone, and let me tell you, it is eating away at your opportunity to prosper and be happy. I know. I have done it. I have looked at people or business mentors and thought that their success came from something other than hard work. Real thoughts I've had:

Well, sure, she's beautiful.

He was rich to start with.

Everybody loves her.

Guess what? This kind of thinking prevents us from being in the present and sticking to our vision. The reason a horse wears blinders in a race is to keep it from watching other horses. So take a cue from the horse: Focus on your race, your life, and your business. The way you change the world is by changing *your* world. Let other people run their race; it has nothing to do with you.

In her book *You Can Heal Your Life*, motivational author and Hay House founder Louise Hay says:

> *Imagine the person in conflict or [who has] envy for you. Then imagine an empty dark movie theatre with a small stage in front of you. See them standing on it. When you can envision them clearly, see and realize all good things coming to them...things that would be meaningful to that person. Hold the image and let it fade away...do this every day. Your life will change and so will theirs.* [p. 91]

If I were to isolate one factor that keeps people stuck and angry, it is blame, and blame is just a form of competition. It's easy to think, "You, it, or that must be the reason I can't make more money. It certainly can't be me." We all do it. Yes, even you.

So, how do we stop doing it? How do we let it go?

First, we start being really honest with ourselves. I love this quote from author and motivational speaker Tony Gaskins, Jr., and while it might piss you off at first, I am hoping it serves as a wakeup call: "Everybody isn't judging you; somebody is telling you the TRUTH!"

Here are three things that could give you a big, fat 180-degree turnaround in the competition breakthrough department:

1. **Listen.** I know it seems like something we learned in kinder-garten, but it's true. Listen. There are some people out there who know way more than you do, and some of it is really cool, deep, smart shit. It can be painful to listen and hear what they have to say, because we live in a world where we're innately defending our choices and ourselves.

   While listening is so important, be sure to listen with a filter; some things won't serve you. You have to get really good at weeding those out, but the things that sting a bit and make sense is the good stuff. If someone or something offends you, then that's when you should pay the most attention. There's a reason it's hitting you so hard; the offense is always within. Listen, filter, and go within. They aren't trying to compete; they are just trying to teach you, so let them.

2. **Take responsibility.** Wherever you are right now in life is a result of your decisions. It's not about your ex-husband or the bad job or the lousy break you got. It is about what you do with all those things—how you respond to them, own them, and use them.

   If you run out of money, don't blame the banks.
   If you run out of time, don't blame your boss.
   If you run out of clients, don't blame your coach.

   Getting responsible means getting results. Don't blame or resent others for what you do not have. You are exactly where you chose to be.

3. **Care less.** The more I learn, the less I care about things—feelings, opinions, results. Don't get me wrong; you won't find too many people that give a damn about stuff as much as I do, but I carefully choose what matters to me. We spend a lot of time in business trying to make people happy and getting them to like us. I find it ironic that the greatest technological connector in the world, Facebook, is based on getting "likes." It's fascinating. Really spend time getting clear on what you care about and what you could care less about.

I've spent the past couple of years on an initiative working with craftswomen in Zimbabwe. It has been both a passion project and the greatest learning experience of my life. When you need to provide the basics to your family, you focus on the now and how to get what you need. It is amazing to see the generosity that these women display. There's no competition. No blame.

I learned a lot from these women, but the greatest lesson was about the power of taking responsibility. You can have all the money and success in the world, but if you choose to blame other people or things, you will always be a hostage to something or someone. Set yourself free to make more money—or simply to enjoy what you already have.

● ● ●

Competition is merely a pathway to quitting. Someone shot off an email to me recently that said, "Not everyone is like you." My reaction: I know, and *thank God!* Can you imagine what that world would look like? Yikes! We were having an exchange about resolve—that ability to go on and on and on and on, to even not see competition because you are so focused on your own opportunity.

I will be the first to tell you that business is messy and it can suck. I mean really suck, sometimes—especially if you are sensitive like I am. Underneath this whip-cracker exterior is someone who cares too much at times, and I often take things personally. Someone leaves or someone doesn't value your program or work, and it can hurt. The really interesting part is the more you serve, the more people quit or complain. And this is what I have a bird's eye view of: *the quitters*.

I know some people prefer to talk about the winners, but I must say, I learn more from the quitters. The winners show up, suck it up, cry, stomp, celebrate, and then rinse and repeat over and over. Every successful entrepreneur I have *ever* coached, been mentored by, or been a colleague to has followed the exact same formula.

The quitters, however, are a bit more interesting.

They are very creative. It's especially interesting to see where and how their particular brand of quitting will appear. Keep in mind that the number-one reason businesses fail is because people simply stop. Yep, stop. I have seen the quitters' cycle firsthand; I have been watching when it starts to creep up on people and kick in. I think it would be useful for people to see the complete trajectory, so they can identify how it starts and how they might stop themselves. There is a huge difference between knowing something needs to come to an end and quitting.

Quitting usually follows this pattern: second-guesses, fear, blame, projecting, feeling overwhelmed, more blame, deciding to quit—then the cycle repeats.

Fascinating, right? I constantly use this paradigm to catch myself and see when I am falling into the cycle. You can honestly use it for anything in your life—going to the gym, building your business, developing a relationship, and so on.

You can catch yourself and get out of this deadly cycle. Then, you can use competition to win, to get to the finish line and inspire others.

Competition comes in three flavors:

1. Healthy competition
2. Self-competition
3. Fear-based competition

Of these three, two are beneficial, and the other will destroy you.

You must be aware of what motivates you, and how you get ahead. When I talk to my clients, they often compare themselves to X person or Y company. They want to know how a colleague or competitor is able to outperform them, close more sales, or expand more quickly. I find it interesting.

I think it is key to get clear about what your goals are and why, so you can figure out what drives the sense of urgency that will bring you motivation.

Be competitive. Be *very* competitive, but be competitive with yourself. Use others only as a litmus test for what you want to do—or what is possible.

Don't view competition as punishment for what you haven't done. Competition can create enthusiasm; it can motivate and inspire. As public servant Henry Chester once said, "Enthusiasm is the greatest asset in the world. It beats money and power and influence. It is no more or less than faith in action."

When you engage in competition based in fear, you are not working for yourself; you are merely looking for others' approval. You're driven by the desire to be liked and needed rather than to reach your own goals. Who are you competing with? How is it motivating you? Do you remember who you are?

Every time I used to leave the house my mom and dad told me, "Remember who you are." I am not sure I understood what they meant 100 percent back then, but now I do. And I've witnessed how important it is in our lives today, especially when it comes to business.

I've noticed an epidemic in business lately. People want to screw people on deals. They want to treat their staff and team like crap, publicly. Not only do they underpay people, but they undervalue them, making it clear that they don't care about their employees. And this brings a mindset that prompts fear of other people's success.

The competition seems so fierce and getting our piece of the pie is so important that we forget who we are. Here's my advice: Treat everyone well.

When I was in college, I remember hearing someone say, "When showing up for an audition, don't be dumb enough to think the person checking you in might not also be auditioning you."

Your client today might be your boss tomorrow. A lower-level colleague might be someone you need tomorrow. Your assistant might become your CEO.

The following three things are worth paying attention to—and worth having.

1. **Have values.** Remember who you are, whether you make it big or not at all. Be kind and be caring. Remember what famed author Maya Angelou said in an interview with Oprah Winfrey: "People will forget what you taught them, but they will never forget how you treated them."

2. **Have manners.** Say thank you and respond to emails. Answer phone calls. Apologize when it's warranted.

3. **Have heart.** Stand up for people who are afraid or confused about how to stand up for themselves. Stand up for people who need someone to have their back. As Martin Luther King, Jr., said in the Trumpet of Conscience speech (1967): "In the end, we will remember not the words of our enemies, but the silence of our friends." Be a friend to those in need and your life will be richer.

Fearful competition affects every element of your business, from your assistant to your customers. Healthy competition puts you in the place you need to be in order to grab an opportunity and make a difference. It prompts you to run just a little harder and faster—not because you have to be first, but because it's a damn good view, and you can learn a lot from the others who are leading the pack. Always run with the lead dogs. In whatever situation you are in, business, life, career, or hobby, you have to stick with the head of the pack to make a difference. I have found a secret weapon to harness useful healthy competition and catch up. It's especially helpful when you feel like everyone around you is running faster, earning more, and doing more. It's powerful for those times when you look at your cash flow and you see the dips and challenges that are holding you back. When you look at everything from non-payments to ending payments to sales and launches, where do you usually find the biggest holes? The answer to this question can be your secret weapon: *sales.*

When this is the problem, it means the company is not on the phone, not in networking mode, not connecting—and worst of all, *not* asking! I know you might get sick of asking for the sale, but it is the absolute truth: Asking is the key to success. I know this from my own experience. When I need to ramp up cash flow, or drum up new business, I pick up the phone. Sales is the lifeline of your business.

If you aren't doing this, then you already know why your business isn't growing. It can't be. Even in this age of every technology imaginable, I have not seen anything better than getting in front of people or calling people. Pick up the phone and ask; then we can tweak results.

Competition is invisible if you are asking consistently.

When you feel the negative pangs of competition sneak up, you most likely do not have a marketing problem; you have a math problem. How many people have you asked? How many connections have you made? How much new potential have you brought in the door?

A few years ago, I had an idea for a new division of my company. It was something creative, which I was yearning for. It was also innovative, which always motivates me—and it was really needed, which pays the bills. I saw someone else in my market who offered this service, and he was good at it. You need to be talented and expressive in the realm of video—and this guy was both.

I surmised that I would need to go on a long hunt to find a creative videographer that could compete with this crew. I was certain we had better business systems and marketing; but they had us beat in the artistic department. After thinking through the options of building and hiring, I remembered something I had always taught. (It's funny how easy it is to forget what we teach.) I remembered the idea that *it's better to partner than to compete.*

Fast-forward a couple of years, and that video company and I have built a booming division of my business. We all got what we needed: I got the best creative in the business, and they got great marketing and a solid partner. And in the end, we all made lots more money.

If you can get creative with your competition instead of always worrying about getting ahead, you'll eliminate the fear-based thinking that keeps you stressed and losing. Embrace the motivating kind of thinking that keeps you innovating and pursuing. Never forget to let go of blame; for you are your own biggest competition. If something isn't working, take a look at yourself. Because *the way you do anything is the way you do everything.*

Competition, as the life of trade, is surely a tremendous spur to progress. Those who are pursued—people or businesses—are the most persistent in their efforts to keep ahead. Having competitors at your heels encourages you to constantly be more efficient, innovative, and progressive. Put your pursuers on the payroll.

Chapter 12 Homework

1. Horses wear blinders.

What do you use to stay focused on the race?
What could you use when you find yourself focusing on the wrong stuff?

2. Blame is a form of competition.

How are you using blame to compete?

Who are you blaming?

3. Listening 101.

Do you actively listen to people?

Who do you listen to who actually knows more than you do?

Who offends you? Do you recognize you have lessons to learn from them?

4. Motivated by competition.

What kind of language motivates you?

Do you partake in healthy competition as a way to better yourself, or do you use negative thinking because you're afraid of what others are doing?

5. How do you treat people?

Are you only nice to the people you know are in charge?

How do you treat the lower-level folks?

Who have you not treated as well, and how could giving a little extra love go a long way?

6. Competition versus partners.

Where can you get creative with your competition?

Rather than compete, could you partner up instead?

7. A pop quiz in three parts.

Part 1: When all else fails, what should you do?

Part 2: What is the lifeline of your business?

Part 3: How do you make competition invisible?

Answer: Sales. Sales. Sales.

CHAPTER 13

Mastery

We are what we repeatedly do. Excellence, then, is not an act, but a habit.

—Aristotle

Experts say that if you read just one business book a month, you'll know more than 96 percent of the people around you in a very short period of time.

The sad truth is that most people stop learning as they grow busier and busier. They settle into their lives or businesses, and are often content to know and do just enough to get by. We do very little to advance ourselves as time goes by, unless it's required as part of a professional licensing program or emerges from the sheer desperation to change something like our income. This negatively affects our happiness and limits our access to opportunities.

In his book *Love Is the Killer App: How to Win Business and Influence Friends*, Tim Sanders, Chief Solutions Officer at Yahoo!, says "The books you read today will fuel your earning power tomorrow."

I think the mastery, practice, and learning you take on today will keep you present and profitable. There are three areas you must master in business:

1. Your craft
2. Your management
3. Your customer service

MASTERING YOUR CRAFT

Of the three, this is the process and act most people enjoy. After all, very few people get into business because marketing excites them. We do it to spread our ideas, share our talents, or do something we love.

Here's the rub: We live in the technology age, when competency is no longer enough in business. You can't be merely good at what you do; you need to be excellent *and* you have to maintain your excellence by continuously studying your craft.

I was an opera major in college. I had enough talent to get into one of the best conservatories in the country. Much of the drive I have in business is due to that training. Great female opera singers hit their prime in their thirties and forties, since the voice, mastery, and depth of the instrument just takes that long to develop. Typically, a child will become interested in music or start voice lessons at the age 12 or 13—but their voice won't truly be ready until 25 years later.

Mastery is a commitment combined with patience and consistency. I am a much better coach and marketer than I was just three years ago. I study every day, I implement various approaches, I see what works by watching myself and others—and I continue to develop. I am not a master by any means, but I strive to be on the path of mastery.

Author, musician, and neuroscientist Daniel Levitin wrote in his *New York Times* bestselling book *This is Your Brain on Music* (Plume, 2006) that experts must practice their craft for 10,000 hours to reach the level of mastery.

Here is, specifically, how Malcolm Gladwell puts it in his book *Outliers: The Story of Success* (Little, Brown and Company, 2008):

> *The emerging scientific picture is that 10,000 hours of practice is required to achieve the level of mastery associated with being a world-class expert in anything. In study after study of composers, basketball players, fiction writers, ice skaters, concert pianists, chess players, master criminals, and what have you, this number comes up again and again.*
>
> *Now, how long is ten thousand hours? It is equal to roughly three hours of practice a day, or twenty hours a week, of practice for ten years. Of course some people never reach mastery, which is not really explainable yet. But, no one has found a case in which true world-class expertise was accomplished in less time. It seems that it takes the brain this long to assimilate all that it needs to know to achieve true mastery.*

Your skill or talent is simply that: a God-given skill or talent. Reaching excellence is your choice. You decide how much time you continually put in to master it. It is also about following what you know, and knowing that you know more than you may think. After you rehearse, study, plan, and do over and over, then you really do know.

For example, when boating it is imperative to understand your buoy markers and shore markings. When I bought my first boat, I really didn't know what an education it would be to learn how to safely navigate. I had been traveling the same path for the past month. I clearly knew the areas to travel and routes to take since I'd been boating them almost daily. But what if I had done it in the dark? What if the safety of daylight was taken away? Would I know where to go or would I sink without my safety net?

One beautiful summer night in Maine, we got caught out in the boat late at night and were using a flashlight to navigate lobster buoys and dry land. I freaked. I was trying to remain calm, but I was really scared. I felt as if I had been dropped onto a different planet. My heart was racing and my insecurities abounded. It was as if I had never taken that path and had no clue what to do next. Land look liked water and water looked like land. Where the hell was I?

Fortunately, we managed to find our way, and once I had navigated myself back to land successfully, I made the connection to business.

This is what happens to so many entrepreneurs. When circumstances change, we forget everything we ever knew. We behave just like all the times we have traveled our business paths before.

I *knew exactly* where to go, intuitively. I had done it before. I just let the one change throw me off, which is precisely what happens in business. We know what to do, where to go, and what we need; we just let the hiccups and changes convince us we don't.

The most authentic marketing strategy and approach to attracting clients is embracing our intuition and trusting ourselves to know the path. The most important part of mastery is remembering what you know.

Once you know, you always have it ready, you can't go backwards. You know what you learn. You know what you practice. You know what to use over and over.

If you feel stumped growing your business or frustrated with mastering what you should be doing, go back to the basics and embrace your inner voice.

- **Stop believing you have to do it like others do it.** You are your own unique brand. Grasp the ideas and approaches that work for and resonate with you. Disregard the rest and use your voice, your gifts, and your language to market. Take your own path to mastery.

- **Don't make it complicated.** You know how to get clients; you have traveled this path before. Always remember and remind yourself of that. Look to your current circle: friends, family, colleagues, and community. Sometimes asking people what you know really works.

  As a speaker, I often get an idea or thought, and will teach on it for 15 minutes. Sometimes I have no clue what I said. I have to go back and ask clients or attendees to share notes or ideas regarding what I shared. Sometimes we forget we know and can do so much.

- **Draw on your past success for the present.** Remind yourself of what has worked in the past and leverage that. Ask yourself: How did you get that client? Where did those referrals come from? What brought in money before?

Repeat success. Just because the sun went down doesn't mean you forget your marketing sense or the mastery of your craft. It is already within you. You know what your path is. Embrace your intuition to be ready for what life throws you. That inner voice will navigate you through the business waters to the path to mastery, even in the dark.

MASTERING YOUR MANAGEMENT

You simply must become a master of people, their needs, and their behaviors. I have found managing people to be the most exhilarating and the most complicated part of being in business.

Ken Blanchard, William Oncken Jr., and Hal Burrows wrote a quick but powerful read called *The One Minute Manager Meets the Monkey*. At its core, the book explains that the best way to make people responsible is to give people responsibility. Management is about inspiration. Management is about understanding what motivates people and how they will save you time if you better understand their motivators.

Tons of colleagues and friends told me to skip all the 20-somethings' resumes that came across my desk. "It's just too hard. They are entitled, they are selfish, and they don't stay anywhere long." But I knew different. The members of Generation Y, the Millennials, I encountered did not have a work ethic issue; they had a management issue.

I was determined to understand them, learn what incentivized them, and use their gifts to grow my company. I knew that some of what my colleagues were saying was true. However, I knew a few other things about 20-somethings, too:

- Growing up, they all got a trophy just for participation; thus they believe they deserve a place at the table.
- They do everything together, thus they value teamwork.
- They are constantly connected with technology, thus they value fast connection.
- Social media has made them obsessed with celebrity, thus they value having someone to look up to.

To grow my business to the next level, I needed team players who were self-assured enough to take a seat at the table. I needed them to understand and be excited by technology, and look for mentors who would treat them well and strive to understand them. I had a hunch that, in the right environment, they would work their asses off in return.

I needed Millennials. And I didn't need to change them. I needed to change me.

The way you do anything is the way you do everything.

You have to understand how to manage, but it's just as important to understand what should and should not be managed. I am a born-again believer in delegation. I delegate almost everything to free myself up to do the things that are important. I do my best every day to master the art of delegation.

I was recently in such tunnel-vision delegation mode that I realized I had overdelegated. I had to remind myself of the wonderful Dan

Kennedy mantra, "The marketing is so important that it cannot be left to the marketing department."

You have to market *you*.

You can get support in almost all areas in business, but when just starting out you need to be sure to stay on top of these six crucial tasks:

1. Make the contacts.
2. Initiate the sales calls.
3. Get in front of people.
4. Research who is the perfect person for you to speak to or connect with.
5. Follow up.
6. Maintain relationships and connections.

There are a multitude of reasons why this is the area you should *not* be delegating, but Les Brown sums it up best when he says, "No one will care about your dream as much as you do!"

Figure out what to take off your plate, *but* don't delegate all of the marketing. You are the best representative of *you*! And you certainly cannot delegate without systems.

We have learned a lot about business over the last couple of years. We have learned that we are reinventing the wheel day in and day out. Not only does this cost you time and money; it also costs you the most valued resource of all—talent.

When an employee doesn't have systems to follow or learn from, your team can become very frustrated. I know I'm a control freak, but once systems were in place, even I was able to delegate 95 percent of everything in the business. I felt comfortable having team members step in and follow the systems and procedures we had in place.

So if you don't have them in place already, start keeping systems for everything you do. Keep the files in a central location, preferably in a shared drive or Google document, so your entire team can access them. Of course, not everything will be perfect. There will always be glitches and things that you simply cannot delegate;

but even a partial systems check and delegation allows you to have freedom in your business. And isn't that what entrepreneurship is about, the freedom to make your own decisions and be the director of your time?

Just like having systems for best practices in place, you need to master customer service. It is your life-blood.

My parents met up with us on a trip to visit my sister in Washington, D.C., one year to watch some Georgetown basketball and celebrate a birthday. Coming out of the Verizon Center, my Dad was a little high on the Georgetown win and a Coors Light, and took a spill and broke his arm. I ended up in the emergency room until 4 AM on a Sunday morning. What a marketing lesson that turned out to be!

The people who worked at the hospital were so efficient and so kind. They constantly checked in on us, and went out of their way to answer questions, explain, and make us feel understood. It was an absolute master class in customer service.

The funny part was we are pretty sure they didn't know what they were doing. They didn't cast my father's arm well; two doctors had slightly different stories but then seemed to get on the same page. I actually had to help the intern put the cast on because he seemed a little confused. But we didn't care. We felt so taken care of that we were just thankful. We kept telling ourselves and each other that if my father needed to, he could visit another doctor the next morning once he returned home. We walked through the whole ER to say thanks, and my dad wrote a personal note.

Amazing customer service will disguise a multitude of flaws. I certainly don't suggest you plan to suck and make up for it with candies and well wishes, but you and your business cannot be perfect all the time. No one can. People will forget what you sold them or what you taught them, but they will remember how you treated them.

Just as Zappos CEO Tony Hsieh says, "If you take care of the customer, they don't care what you sell." People want to be taken care of. The product becomes secondary; if you treat your customers well, you can even change your product and people will still be interested in buying.

So, ask yourself these questions:

How do you *take care* of your clients and customers?

How do you overpromise and overdeliver?

If someone asked one of your clients what working with you was like, what do *you* think they would say?

Have you surveyed your clients or customers to find out how they feel served?

What is one (even little) thing you can do this week to make your followers, clients, or customers feel *really* taken care of?

I am all for people being made to feel good. This is why I stress this point: You may not know everything yet or be an expert or have perfected your product; but if you lead your customers and clients with care and attention, they will follow. I just hope you don't have to end up in the ER to learn the lesson!

• • •

When you find something that works, *keep doing it*! Replication is the key.

As painful, fun, scary, insane, and by-the-seat-of-your-pants it all is, keep doing what works. Even if it worked just a little, repeat, repeat, repeat. That is what successful business owners do differently. They don't keep launching new things. They grow, expand, develop, and focus on the successes. They master what works and what is already done before creating. Sell what you have created before you create what is next.

I learned the lesson the hard way. I launched a bright, new, shiny program and it confused the hell out of my subscribers.

So look at your revenue right now. Whether you are making $5 or $5 million, where is most of that income coming from? Focus there and grow, grow, grow.

MAKE TIME FOR LIFE

One of my very first private clients asks this question on her website: "Do you pop up like toast in the morning?"

I popped out of bed this morning for a few reasons. I have several clients whom I adore, and one in particular always gives me clarity and energy. I love watching him succeed. I am also excited by my day full of planning and working with my team, and I have a big idea I can't wait to put in place.

I will take the boat out later today, but not before checking on the progress of the new house we are building. I am going out to dinner and a movie tonight. And finally I need to put finishing touches on a girl getaway to Napa and the flights for my Africa trip.

My business is very busy. My life is very fulfilling. How are you waking up to face your day? Is it all business and no play?

The question people ask me most is: How do I stay motivated in my life and in my business? Here is the answer: You will *never* need to ask that question in the first place if you're doing business that you love and living a life that you love. Remember back in eighth grade when you were in deep infatuation with that boy or girl? You didn't remind yourself to wait by their locker. You didn't remind yourself to call them or wait for them after school. You didn't have to remind yourself to pass them a note in class. You just did it because you were infatuated and in love.

So, what's stopping you from falling in love with your *life*!?

Make time for your life. You can't fall in love with anything you don't make time for. Not your business, and certainly not your life. It takes time to get good at things. Business gets better when your life gets richer.

In the end, time is all we really have. I can make more money. I can get more help. I can even get some do-overs; but I can't make more time or get back lost time. Figure out your time wasters, time drains, and time fears and clean them up. Because the more time you take, the less money you make.

Chapter 13 Homework

1. **Mastering your craft.**

   How are you working to further master your craft?

   Are you dedicated to mastering *beyond* what is expected of you? What was the last book you read on your specialty? The last time you took a course?

2. **Ten thousand hours to expertise.**

   How many hours have you put in on your path to mastery? Seriously.

   How much time do you think you've really put into the business you offer?

   How much could you improve by going even further?

3. **Mastering your management.**

   Do you have a team?

   How do you manage their activities and their expectations?

   How do you handle conflicts?

   How do you inspire?

   Do you know what motivates them?

   Do you know what to delegate and what to hold on to?

4. **Mastering customer service.**

   How do you treat your customers?

   Do you have a process for how you handle customer inquiries and purchases?

   Do you underpromise and overdeliver—or the other way around?

   Have you ever messed up with clients and made good?

5. **Mastering your life.**

   Are you in love with your life?

   What does your business do to support your life? What does it allow and afford you to do?

CHAPTER 14

Plan

Dreams don't come true. Plans come true.

—Larry Winget

Every time I hold a retreat or event, people always enter with the same enthusiastic desire for an outcome: clarity. They want clarity, they need clarity, and they crave clarity. But clarity only comes from one place: planning.

I know that many people out there have a lot of responsibility assigned to them. You know you need to do, you can't do it all at once, and you can't do it alone. Everything must be in order and in time.

I think the biggest cause of "business paralysis" is that we have too much to do, so we do nothing. We actually plan to fail.

How do I overcome business paralysis? Well, here's my little trick, in five simple steps:

1. For a short period, I give each of my projects an even amount of time as if I were doing them all at warp speed. This typically lasts two to four weeks.

2. Then, I go to the calculator and figure out what project has the most impact on my bottom line. I put the projects in order of priority.

3. Next, I pull out my year-long strategy and determine my three end goals for the year in each of the below categories:

   • Money
   • Impact
   • Lifestyle

4. I then ask myself whether the order in which I now have the projects aligns with the cash flow order and my three goals.

   If the answer is yes, I set end dates and move forward.

   If no, I take another look and see where the puzzle pieces need to shift.

5. Finally, I get going on the list order.

Do not miss your own deadlines. If that means getting help, jobbing it out, getting three coaches to kick your ass, then so be it. Get it done. You do not miss the deadlines you set for yourself.

As my friend and mentor David Neagle told me, "If you lie to yourself enough times, you won't believe anything you say."

The more deadlines you miss, the less you'll believe in yourself and your ability to meet your goals. Planning is essential in business and meeting deadlines is critical.

There are entire companies dedicated to planning and solutions, but the bottom line is this: You need a simple formula that allows you to make good decisions fast.

My 10k program leads business owners through a year of training, strategy, and planning. After years of coaching and observing business, I saw the same theme over and over: a business plan of attack could only be sustained about every 60 days. It would inevitably happen again and again, starting around day 57: I'd see people losing steam, losing faith, and losing clarity.

We need a plan, a new, revised plan, about every 60 days. And while every entrepreneur is different, a vast majority of us are high-energy, high-strung, and easily distractible. We take risks and we launch and learn. A plan needs to reflect that by being modified every two months. So make a plan to plan.

Just like money, clients, and success, plans don't just happen. You have to plan to plan. Make and schedule the time you need for your ideas to take hold. Most business owners have a passion, a good idea, or a skill and they get inspired to monetize. That's always the seed of a great startup.

But most startups fail because business owners believe that their passion will somehow magically "bring them" the money. Passion will inspire you to work hard and get you out of bed in the morning; but you need a solid plan based in 10 percent information and 90 percent implementation.

When you have a plan, you are able to scale your model and profit centers. Then you simply rinse and repeat. Here is my five-step plan to make money, every day, every time.

1. **Ask where?**

   When you plan a project, launch, or product, know from the start where you want it to take you, both financially and in terms of how it will affect your position. It is essential to have an overall plan for the year so that you see each launch or idea fits in, and the impact each will have. Most people simply throw the spaghetti on the wall and hope something sticks, but it is imperative that you ask where this is going to take you. It is vital to have a clear and measurable outcome.

2. **Ask when?**

   What are your set dates for the most successful profit outcome? Once you determine those, you have to live and die by them. When you miss launch dates, you throw off your entire profit cycle.

3. **Ask who?**

   Speaker, author, and coach Loral Langmeir had a phenomenal quote: "When an opportunity comes to you, ask yourself the million-dollar question: Who can I get to do this for me?"

   You must leverage your time as soon as possible, even if you are just starting out. Have a team of resources, contractors, or employees to carry out the tasks and technical work, so you can do what you do best.

4. **Analyze and test.**

   Everything I do or undertake—every email, call, newsletter, or event—is a test. We are constantly analyzing our results and improving upon what worked, changing what didn't, and eliminating waste. If you don't analyze and test your results from start to finish, you are marketing in a vacuum.

5. **Play big and plan small.**

   Most companies focus on the big end result, or their five-year plan. While it's necessary to take a "big-picture" view for some things, some people become so consumed with the big picture that they can't figure out what to do *right now*. When you're looking for doable, step-by-step, sustainable results that can be tested, don't plan further out than 60 days. Your results truly are the indicator of what next step to take.

Nano-planning allows for flexibility and achievable results. Neither hope nor passion is a business plan. They just enable you to work the plan. Plan to be strong and solid.

We are all being recruited all the time. Walk through the airport, and you'll be recruited for credit cards. Visit church with a friend, you'll be recruited to come back. Walk through the mall, and Auntie Anne's will recruit you to have a pretzel sample. It is in our nature as human beings to recruit. We are not solitary human beings, which is why, whether you believe it or not, everyone is born with an innate ability to sell.

Stop for a moment and think about who is recruiting you. I constantly see individuals who don't show up, want to quit, and don't ask for help. They find it easier to recruit other people to believe the same as they do. They claim that a program or plan isn't working, and say, "It's not your fault. It's the coach, the program, the people, the style."

I get it. Misery loves company. When you aren't getting the results you want, you would rather it be someone else's fault. It's preferable to blame something outside of yourself, instead of your own inaction or cycle of quitting. We want to feel like we are a part of something bigger. So when you have that spouse, friend, or colleague telling you *why* something is not or will not work for you, ask these questions:

- Is this individual taking 100 percent responsibility for himself?
- Am I taking 100 percent responsibility for myself?
- If quitting were not even an option, what would my next step be?
- How does this gossip help me?
- How can I support this person? People in deep pain recruit others to fail or quit with them.

Then, determine where this person is in the cycle of quitting.

Remember that we are always being recruited. Sometimes, it can be fun, but it can also be intellectual bullying disguised as support when someone tries to stop your experience or qualify why it will not work for you. When that happens, just ask yourself the questions above, pause, breathe, and reach for support and perspective. As my good friend Matthew Goldfarb says all the time, "It's ok to fit in, but it's better to stand out."

Plan to be strong.

Plan to work your plan.

Plan not to stop.

Plan to plan.

Plan to rest.

Now get out your calendar. Begin to look through your quarterly schedule. Do you have a vacation or personal retreat booked every three to four months? If you wanted only one week off a year, you could have stayed in a day job, but you are an entrepreneur. You are your boss! You are in charge, and we made these choices to live. We made this decision to serve others, but also to serve ourselves, to gain the life we wanted.

Take a nice breath in.

Exhale. Again. Now, ask yourself:

What do you want your life to look like?

What is *most* important to you?

What's on your to-do-before-you-die list?

All of ours will be different. Mine lists travel, food, family, volunteering, and being near the water. Write yours down.

Now, every three to four months I want you to block out a minimum of five to seven days (yep, you heard me) to live that dream. Go ahead. It's an assignment.

For some it will be staying home with family (no work), or taking a trip to the beach. For some, a dream trip to Greece or a month off in Italy. You might choose to take a pottery class or go on a cooking tour. Some people will cycle through Europe, and others will adopt a child. Is volunteering in Haiti on your list? How about a road trip? Some people will hike a mountain, and others will plan a spa and shopping week. Some people will not spend a dime and some will spend too much! But there will be two things in common for everyone:

1. Take off five to seven days EVERY three to four months.
2. If you follow through, your business will be stronger because of it.

What do you *love*? Who do you love doing it with? I look at my partner, my family, and my friends, and this year has reminded me nothing is promised.

Get out your calendar, and plan your life to the extent I ask you to plan your business. None of us will lie on our deathbed and wish we had spent more time on our emails or follow-up calls.

Your life is waiting. Nothing is promised. Nothing happens by accident. Miracles are simply plans put into action. So get planning.

Chapter 14 Homework

1. **Plan your dream.**

   What's your dream?
   What's the plan to make that dream happen?
   Great, now get off your ass and do it.

2. **Deadlines for your deadlines.**

   Do you miss your own deadlines?
   Why? What's the holdup?

What's the one thing you can change right now to stop the nonsense and get shit done?

3. **Your 60-day plan.**

Do you have one? Or are you relying on hope to make sure things just kind of happen?

4. **Five to seven days every three to four months.**

Are you prepared to take off five to seven days every three to four months?

If not, why? What do you think will go wrong?

How happier might you be if you planned in a little play?

CHAPTER 15

Love

I have decided to stick with love. Hate is too great a burden to bear.

—Martin Luther King, Jr.

Do you know what a *lull* is?

My friend Brandon Tuss says that if you're having a party, the fifth time the room or table goes silent, then the party is over. Those silences are lulls, and lulls can compromise your business just as easily as your dinner party.

Not too long ago, I felt a few lulls in my business, and it was getting pretty close to five times in a row. I was at that moment where you don't jump up with enthusiasm at the task and your job does not have the feeling it used to.

The greatest business asset we can all have is tenacity. It's not marketing, not sales, not anything but the commitment to stay in the game. You might fall out of love with your business, but you have to come back to it and stay until you fall back *in* love.

You stay the course when you are in love, and you stay the course when you are not in love.

Answer two things, and keep it short and simple:

1. I am committed to _____.
2. Without fail, over the next seven days I will _____.

Now, *hold the intention* for this to happen.

If you decide to abandon your business or a plan every time you fall out of love you with it, you will never gain any real traction. There will be days with passion, and there will be days you can't find the love anywhere, but no matter what kind of day it is, you must be consistent.

And something else you must do: *Stop watching others.* They have nothing to do with you. Do you constantly look at what other people have—from their homes and cars, to their spouses and partners—and think "I wish I had *that*"?

Hey! Stop watching others.

It's costing you emotionally, energy-wise. You will always feel behind, you will always feel a little bit bitter, and you will always feel like everybody else is doing something that you're not doing.

So stop letting this distract you. Put your blinders on and focus on what *you* are doing.

I don't care if you're making 100 bucks or 100 million. Worry about you, eliminate thoughts about what everybody else is doing, and allow yourself to set your own goals and your own pace.

It might sound crazy, but I don't see that there is any competition. I'm not concerned with what other folks are doing. I'm focused on what we are doing here at Suzanne Evans Coaching. I'm focused on how we can grow today. I'm focused on how we can run our own race today.

I know you may not want to admit it, but you are worried about other people. The competition looks super sexy, and when you slip out of love it's easy to lose focus. Here's my advice: Love the one you're with. Love *your* life.

In a speech at Wright State University, Anna Quindlen said, "You cannot be really first-rate at your work if your work is all you are." As I read this quote today, I was reminded of what makes us powerful entrepreneurs and business owners: blurring the lines of life and business!

There is a difference between a workaholic and an entrepreneur. We choose entrepreneurship for freedom and forwardness. We have the freedom to do it our way and to forge our own path, and the forwardness to use whatever style and message serves us. There is beauty in combining work, pleasure, leisure, and fun. I love the ideas of all the blurred lines so that my entire life seems directed by choice and passion. But here's a business tip: If your work becomes *all* that you are, no one will care about your business. You can't be the best you can be without being diverse and interesting, and constantly experiencing new things.

Take five minutes and write a list of all that you are beyond your business, then take a close look at the truth:

How hard are you playing in those areas?

Which ones are you neglecting?

Work hard, play harder. If you combine them, you will prosper.

People notice love. People both in and out of your industry talk. They compare notes and remember.

When going on your quests to get partners, investors, or joint ventures, remain aware that the experience will be repeated and shared over and over again. So remain professional, be timely, and be pleasant.

People notice when you love what you do, and love those you do it with. It goes back to the lessons we learned in kindergarten: Don't forget to say please and thank you, and remember to play fair. I can't tell you how many colleagues and friends will say, "No, don't partner with that person because he didn't send an email, or she didn't follow through." Do what you say you will because it will come back around. Love people, or get out of business.

It deserves repeating: The way we do anything is the way we do everything. So spread the love.

LOVE HELPING OTHERS

Zig Ziglar said that the fastest way to get rich is to help others get rich. If you spend time connecting, supporting, and promoting other people, your exposure and impact will rise rapidly.

So, keep asking, "Who can I help today?" Don't worry about who gets the credit for success. Just work on making everyone successful. Then, out of the blue, and often by surprise, you too will be successful. There is plenty of success to go around, and it is blissful to have the power to pass it out.

LOVE WHO YOU ARE

I've never fit in. I refuse to try.

I *did* try because, for the first 30 years of my life, I didn't really know any different.

At seven years old, I skipped slumber parties if they were the same night as *60 Minutes*, and at six I gave a political speech for Geraldine Ferraro. None of my friends knew who she was. As I grew older,

I couldn't have cared less about high school gossip, so instead I spent the summers training as a professional water-skier.

Don't get me wrong. I wanted to hang with the cool kids, and I did. I could get along with anybody. I like people, so I got along with the nerds, hung out with the preps, and spent the weekend with the dreadlocked hippy group at school. But I never really *fit* anywhere. Believe me, I would try. I was extremely malleable so I would shift and change and try to be whoever I needed to in that moment. It never really worked.

I have been bossy since age three. I have been overweight since I was five. I have always been the girl who does a little of everything. I wasn't fitting in, and I floundered between being deeply bothered and feeling total apathy. Then I turned 32.

I noticed I was a pretty good marketer. I saw ideas that some people didn't. I had the primal urge to rage against what everybody else was saying, writing, and selling, and do it a little differently. I like a good challenge. I like to poke people. Then it hit me: My marketing works *because* I don't fit in.

Suddenly, I had clarity, and resolved:

- I won't even try to fit in (not even a little).
- I will not stop cursing.
- I will not behave the way you think a coach should or a marketer should or a conscious entrepreneur should.
- I will not make you feel good by telling you BS.
- I will not run my business off of emotional business management (EBM) in the same way that entrepreneurs have for years.
- I will not sell the way everyone else does.
- I will not be feminine or masculine, hardcore or "heart–core."
- I will not do what my industry does because it looks good or is polite.
- I will be me. I don't fit in, and it works.

And I invite you to join me!
I don't want you to fit in, either.

Many people remember when actress Sally Field won the best actress Oscar in 1984 and squealed, "You like me. You really like me!"

Many of you are doing that very same thing in your business. Maybe it happens when you get a client, or at networking groups, or in your masterminds, or even in your marketing copy. You want to be liked. You *need* to be liked. And it is keeping you broke.

I have long said I do what I do to make a difference, not to make friends, and it has allowed me to be unattached to the outcomes. Martha Beck (the very wise life coach for *O*) says, "I love you, but I don't care what you do." I think that's brilliant.

The moment I care what you do, the moment I care if you love me, my capacity for growth ends.

You see, to truly make a difference and be of service you have to be clear that the work is more important than the attention. Here are three fast tracks to focusing on what matters so you can make more money:

1. **Stop worrying about what happened in high school.**

    I know it sucked for lots of people, but it is over. Get over it. This is business, and no one is running for prom queen. We are running for profits. The need to be the most popular might get you invited to parties, but it won't get you rich. Time and energy spent in this area force you to make bad decisions because you are in protection mode instead of progress mode.

2. **Be a bitch or bastard or blowhard or whatever.**

    If you have something to say, then *say it*, dammit! Even if you think saying it will make you come off as one of those dreaded B-words. Own your point of view and be willing to piss people off to have your message heard. You are smart! I'm not telling you to wander around and be a bully; just stop caring whose feathers you might ruffle. You know the difference. Share your point of view!

3. **Don't get your love solely from your business.**

    If you are doing what you are doing for want of attention or fame, then *stop!* You are going to be miserable; chances are, you already are. Your business cannot fulfill your emptiness. It cannot give you enough attention to feel whole or special. It *can* bring you joy, light, or purpose, but it cannot bring you love.

I know this might sound harsh, but I don't care. I love you, but I do not care what you do. I will support you. I will help you. I will love you, but the moment I attach my needs of love or acceptance on you, I have failed you.

So take a moment of truth: Do you need people to love you?

If you said yes, you found your money block. On the other side is freedom.

The why of why your business isn't making more money is that you want to be loved more than you love yourself. If you don't love yourself and your business, then no one else will. The way you do anything is the way you do everything.

Chapter 15 Homework

1. **Love the one you're with.**

   Do you love your business?

   Why? What do you actually love about it?

   Do you hate your business? If so, do you *really* hate it, or are you just in a lull?

   What would make you fall in love again?

2. **Be more than your business.**

   I asked earlier for you to list all the ways that you are more than your business. Get that list. I am not asking you to do anything else, but it's so damn important I want to make sure you don't gloss that over.

3. Who can you help today?

List three to five people you can show a little love today without asking anything in return. You'll be surprised at the results.

4. Love who you are.

Do you like yourself?

Do you care what others think?

Are you content with who you are? (I'm not asking about *where* you are in life, but *who* you are as a person.)

5. How do you stand out?

What makes you different?

Do you need people to love you?

What do you tolerate?

What don't you tolerate?

What will you never do?

Index

FEELING STUCK?

Get Suzanne's best advice uncensored, sarcastic, and to the point about why you're stuck and how to make a big change fast. In an exclusive chapter so "Suzanne" the publishers didn't send it to print, learn what's holding you back. Warning: only download this chapter if you are willing to hear the whole truth. It's aggressive. It's jarring. And it works.

   To download this chapter now, visit thewayyoudoanything.com/secretchapter or scan this QR code: